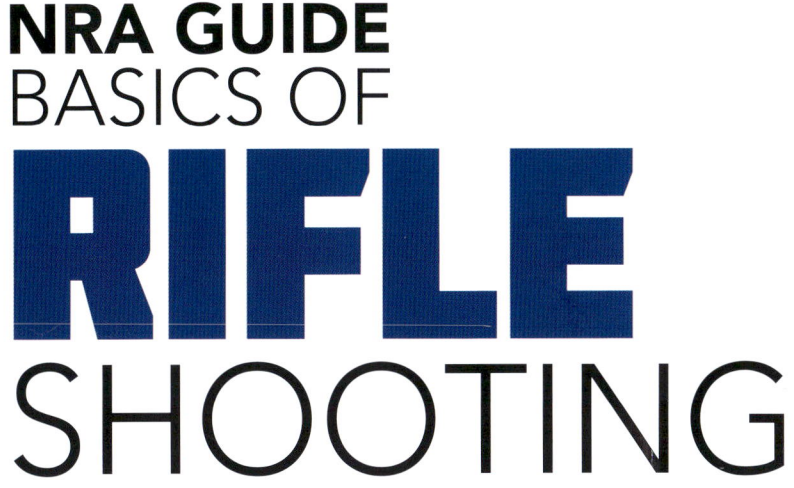

NRA GUIDE
BASICS OF
RIFLE
SHOOTING

Produced by the Education & Training Division

A Publication of the National Rifle Association of America

Second Edition—July 2015
Copyright 2015 The National Rifle Association of America

International Standard Book Number (ISBN): 978-0-935998-29-0

All rights reserved. Printed in the United States of America.
This book may not be reproduced in whole or in part by mechanical means, photocopying, electronic reproduction, scanning, or any other means without written permission. For information, write: Training Department, Education & Training Division, National Rifle Association of America, 11250 Waples Mill Road, Fairfax, VA 22030.

NR40830EF13182   7-16

DISCLAIMER

The NRA expressly disclaims any and all liabilities, losses, costs, claims, remands, suits or actions of any type or nature whatsoever, arising from or in any way related to: this manual; the use of this manual; any representation, drawing or statement made in this manual; or any claim that a particular action is in compliance or performed in accordance or pursuant to this manual.

This manual is under no circumstances to be viewed as a restatement of the law in any jurisdiction or to assure compliance with any applicable federal, state or local laws, ordinances, rules or regulations. You must consult a local attorney to ascertain compliance with all applicable federal, state or local laws, ordinances, rules or regulations and to advise you of the applicable duty of care required of firearms instructors in your jurisdiction.

Instructors should consult with their attorneys for advice on reducing their potential liability for injuries or damages which students or others may incur while learning to use rifles safely, or as a result of other activities. The effectiveness of theories of liability (e.g., strict liability, negligence and others) and methods for protecting oneself from liability (e.g., incorporation, waivers and others) vary between different jurisdictions, and the attorney consulted should be familiar with the law of the applicable jurisdiction.

Discharging firearms in poorly ventilated areas, cleaning firearms, or handling ammunition or lead-containing reloading components may result in exposure to lead. Have adequate ventilation at all times. Wash hands with water after exposure.

Great pains have been taken to make this book as complete as possible; however, it is designed to be used in conjunction with the classroom and firing range instruction of the NRA Basic Rifle Shooting Course. Reading this guide is not, in itself, sufficient to confer proficiency in rifle shooting, safety and maintenance. The reader of this book should obtain additional knowledge and hands-on training.
Visit nrainstructors.org to find courses near you.

TABLE OF CONTENTS

Safety Note viii
Introduction ix

PART I: SAFETY
Chapter 1: Basic Firearm Safety 3
Chapter 2: Safe Firearm Storage 7

PART II: RIFLE MECHANISMS AND OPERATION
Chapter 3: Introduction to Rifle Mechanisms 13
Chapter 4: Bolt-Action Rifle Parts and Operation 19
Chapter 5: Semi-Automatic Rifle Parts and Operation 29
Chapter 6: Lever-Action Rifle Parts and Operation 39
Chapter 7: Slide-Action Rifle Parts and Operation 47
Chapter 8: Other Types of Rifle Actions 55
Chapter 9: Ammunition Fundamentals 59
Chapter 10: Clearing Common Rifle Stoppages 65

PART III: BUILDING RIFLE SHOOTING SKILLS
Chapter 11: Fundamentals of Rifle Shooting 69
Chapter 12: Fundamentals of Rifle Shooting Positions 75
Chapter 13: The Benchrest Position 79
Chapter 14: The Standing Position 85
Chapter 15: The Prone Position 89
Chapter 16: The Kneeling Position 93
Chapter 17: The Sitting Position 97

PART IV: RIFLE SHOOTING ACTIVITIES
Chapter 18: Rifle Shooting Activities 103
Chapter 19: Additional Opportunities for Skill Development 113

PART V: RIFLE SELECTION AND MAINTENANCE
Chapter 20: Selecting Rifles, Ammunition and Accessories 119
Chapter 21: Cleaning and Maintaining Your Rifle 127

APPENDIXES
Appendix A: Using the Sling 137
Appendix B: Using the Shotgun as a Rifle 141
Appendix C: Facts About the NRA 145
Index 149

SAFETY NOTE

The NRA's first and most fundamental Rule for Safe Gun Handling is **<u>ALWAYS</u> keep the gun pointed in a safe direction.** This rule must always be observed; it cannot be relaxed even for legitimate education or training purposes. Absolute, unvarying adherence to this most important of gun safety rules cannot be overemphasized.

In some of the photographs in this book that illustrate specific shooting stances or positions, it was sometimes necessary, for instructional purposes, to position the camera in front of the muzzle of the gun. At no time was an actual functioning firearm used in these photographs; special deactivated, non-firing training guns, or solid plastic gun simulators, were employed, and in some cases, the camera was activated by a remote trigger.

What you should expect when you attend the NRA Basic Rifle Shooting Course

The course goal is to teach the basic knowledge, skills, and attitude for owning and operating a rifle safely.

You should expect at least eight hours of instruction, which includes classroom and range time learning to shoot rifles. You will learn NRA's rules for safe gun handling; rifle parts and operation; ammunition; shooting fundamentals; range rules; shooting from the bench rest position; cleaning the rifle; and continued opportunities for skill development. To earn a certificate, you should be able to consistently shoot acceptable groups on a one-inch bullseye target at 50 feet if rimfire is used, and six inch bullseye at 100 yards if centerfire is used. Students will receive the NRA guide to the Basics of Rifle Shooting handbook, NRA Gun Safety Rules card, Winchester/NRA Marksmanship Qualification booklet, take a Basics of Rifle Shooting Student Examination, and receive a course completion certificate.

Please contact the NRA Training Department at nrainstructors@nrahq.org if you have any comments or concerns regarding your NRA Basic Rifle Shooting course.

INTRODUCTION

The word *rifle* may come from the Old French *rifler*, which means "to scratch." Another possible origin is the Low German word *riffel*, or *groove*. Support for this latter origin is found in the fact that breech-to-muzzle spiral grooves were introduced in Germanic arms in the late 1400s.

The main benefit of the rifled bore is the spin imparted to the bullet, which gives it gyroscopic stability to enhance accuracy. Despite this benefit, widely recognized by the 15th century, rifled bores did not quickly supplant smoothbore muskets. Rifled-barrel guns were more difficult to load, fouled more quickly and were more expensive to produce than muskets, all of which postponed the wide acceptance of rifles among the military until the 19th century. Once adopted, however, rifled-barrel shoulder arms revolutionized military tactics and effectively changed the course of history.

As a general definition, a rifle is a firearm having a relatively long barrel and a stock that fits against the shoulder. Many different types of rifles may be encountered, including bolt-actions, semi-automatics, lever-actions, pump-actions, and several kinds of single-shot guns. All are discussed in this book, although the main focus is on the first four of these types.

Not covered in this book are muzzleloading rifles. In recent decades, interest in shooting these unique guns has increased significantly. Almost all states allow hunting with muzzleloaders, and each year more and more people become involved in shooting these rifles. To learn about muzzleloading rifles, see the NRA How-To Series publication *Muzzleloading*.

Air rifle shooting is also a very popular activity. An air gun utilizes compressed air or other gas (such as CO_2) to propel a lead pellet out the bore. This type of shooting can provide a wide variety of recreation and sport opportunities, from shooting in a basement or backyard range to competing in the Olympic Games.

Americans own rifles today for many different reasons. Many rifle owners engage in various types of hunting. Others compete in the various types of rifle shooting matches held throughout the country and the world, including those held at Olympic level. Still others own rifles for home protection, pest control, or the simple joy of informal target practice, or plinking.

A new shooter will quickly discover that rifle shooting is fun! It is a sport that requires good hand/eye coordination, mental concentration and discipline. The purpose of this book is to teach the safe and proper use of a rifle so that it can be enjoyed to the fullest extent.

The main focus of *The NRA Guide to the Basics of Rifle Shooting* is on helping the reader develop the knowledge, skills and attitude to safely and effectively handle and fire a rifle. Included are chapters on ammunition and rifle types; selecting ammunition, rifles and accessories; gun handling; shooting positions; and rifle shooting activities. These and other topics presented in this book form the core knowledge and skills used in all rifle shooting activities, from informal recreational shooting through hunting, competition and home protection.

Although this book has a wealth of information on many aspects of rifle use, it is meant to be used within the framework of the NRA Basic Rifle Shooting Course, a program encompassing eight hours of classroom and range instruction. It is also used to support the NRA FIRST Steps Course. You should understand that merely reading a book—any book—will not, in itself, make you proficient in handling and using a rifle.

> ### A Gun Owner's Responsibilities
>
> Americans enjoy a right that citizens of many other countries do not—the right to own firearms. But with this right come responsibilities. It is the gun owner's responsibility to store, operate and maintain his or her firearms safely. It is the gun owner's responsibility to ensure that unauthorized or untrained individuals cannot gain access to his or her firearms. And it is the gun owner's responsibility to learn and obey all applicable laws that pertain to the purchase, possession and use of a firearm in his or her locale. Guns are neither safe nor unsafe by themselves. When gun owners learn and practice responsible gun ownership, guns are safe.

ACKNOWLEDGEMENTS

The NRA would like to thank the many NRA staff, NRA Certified Instructors, NRA members, and others whose efforts and participation helped make the development and production of this book possible.

PART I

SAFETY

CHAPTER 1
Basic Firearm Safety

Safety is fundamental to all shooting activities. Whether you're practicing at the range, hunting in the field, or cleaning your gun in your workshop, the rules of firearm safety always apply.

Safe gun handling involves the development of *knowlege, skills,* and *attitude* — knowledge of the gun safety rules, the skill to apply these rules, and a safety-first attitude that arises from a sense of responsibility and an understanding of potential dangers.

Most gun accidents are caused by *ignorance* and/or *carelessness*. Ignorance is a lack of knowledge— a person who handles a gun without knowing the gun safety rules or how to operate the gun is exhibiting a dangerous lack of knowledge. Equally dangerous is the person who, although knowing the gun safety rules and how to properly operate a gun, becomes careless in properly applying this knowledge. In both of these cases, accidents can happen. When people practice responsible ownership and safe use of guns; accidents *don't* happen.

Though there are many specific principles of safe firearm operation, all are derived from just three basic, safe gun handling rules.

ALWAYS keep the gun pointed in a safe direction.

FUNDAMENTAL RULES FOR SAFE GUN HANDLING

<u>ALWAYS</u> keep the gun pointed in a safe direction.

This is the primary rule of gun safety. A safe direction means that the gun is pointed so that even if it were to go off, injury or damage would be avoided. The key to this rule is to control where the muzzle or front end of the barrel is pointed at all times. Common sense dictates the safest direction, depending upon the circumstances. At the range, a "safe direction" is downrange. If only this one safety rule were always followed, there would be no injuries or damage from unintentional discharges.

<u>ALWAYS</u> keep your finger off the trigger until ready to shoot.

Your trigger finger should always be kept straight, alongside the rifle's receiver or stock and out of the trigger guard, until you have made the decision to shoot. Unintentional discharges can be caused when the trigger

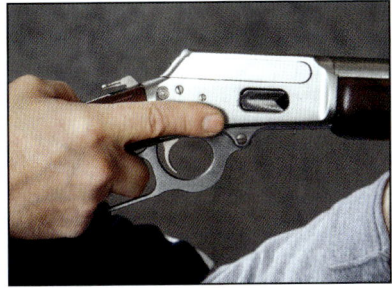

ALWAYS keep your finger off the trigger until ready to shoot.

Chapter 1: Basic Firearm Safety

ALWAYS keep the gun unloaded until ready to use.

of a loaded gun is inadvertently pressed by a finger left in the trigger guard instead of being positioned straight along the side of the gun's receiver or stock.

<u>ALWAYS</u> keep the gun unloaded until ready to use.

A firearm that is not being used should always be unloaded. For example, at the range your firearm should be left unloaded with the action open while you walk downrange to check your target. Similarly, a firearm that is stored in a gun safe or gun case should always be unloaded.

As a general rule, whenever you pick up a gun, point it in a safe direction with your finger off the trigger, engage the safety, if present, remove the ammunition, open the action and visually and physically inspect the chamber to determine if the gun is loaded or not. Unless the firearm is being kept in a state of readiness for home protection, it should be unloaded. If you do not know how to open the action or inspect the firearm, leave the gun alone and get help from someone who does. Further information on rifle mechanisms will be presented in Part II: Rifle Mechanisms and Operation.

RULES FOR USING OR STORING A GUN

In addition to these three fundamental Rules for Safe Gun Handling, you need to observe a number of additional rules when you use or store your firearm.

Know your target and what is beyond.

Whether you are at the range or in the woods, if you're going to shoot, you must know what lies beyond your target. In almost all cases, you must be sure that there is something that will serve as a backstop to capture bullets that miss or go through the target. You must **NEVER** fire in a direction in which there are people, buildings, vehicles or anything else that may be threatened by errant gunfire. Think first, shoot second.

Know how to use the gun safely.

Before handling a gun, learn how it operates. Read the owner's manual for your gun; contact the manufacturer for an owner's manual if you do not have one. Know your gun's basic parts, how to safely open and close the action, and how to remove ammunition from it. No matter how much you know about guns, you must always take the time to learn the proper way to operate any new or unfamiliar firearm. Never assume that because one gun resembles another, they both operate similarly. Also, remember that a gun's mechanical safety is never foolproof. Guidance in safe gun operation should be obtained from the owner's manual or a qualified firearm instructor or gunsmith.

Most rifles of a particular type (such as bolt- or pump-actions) work in essentially the same way, allowing an individual familiar with one model to be likely to know how to operate another of the same type. Nonetheless, it is still essential for you to be thoroughly familiar with the proper operating procedure for your particular rifle.

Be sure your gun is safe to operate.

Just like other tools, guns need regular maintenance. Proper cleaning and storage are a part of the gun's general upkeep. If there is any question regarding a gun's ability to function, it should be examined by a knowledgeable gunsmith. Proper maintenance procedures are found in your owner's manual.

Use only the correct ammunition for your gun.

Each firearm is intended for use with a specific cartridge. Only cartridges designed for a particular gun can be fired safely in that gun. Most rifles have the ammunition type stamped on the barrel or, less commonly, on the frame or receiver. The owner's manual will also list the cartridge or cartridges appropriate for your gun. Ammunition can be identified by information printed on the cartridge box and usually stamped on the cartridge head. Do not shoot the gun unless you absolutely know you have the proper ammunition.

Note that there are some rifle cartridges that have more than one name, such as the 6 mm Remington and .244 Remington. Moreover, there are a handful of rifle cartridges that are physically interchangeable, but which operate at different pressure levels; the commercial .223 Rem. and military 5.56 mm are examples of these. Always ensure that you are using the proper ammunition for your rifle.

Wear eye and ear protection as appropriate.

The sound of a gunshot can damage unprotected ears. Gun discharges can also emit debris and hot gas that could cause eye injury. Thus, both ear and eye protection are highly recommended whenever you are firing live ammunition in your gun. Safety glasses and ear plugs or muffs should also be worn by any spectators or shooting partners present during live-fire sessions.

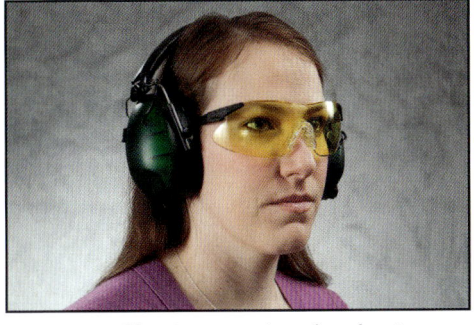

Wear eye and hearing protection when shooting.

Never use alcohol or drugs before or while shooting.

Alcohol and many drugs can impair normal mental and physical bodily functions, sharply diminishing your ability to use a gun safely. These substances must never be used before or while handling or shooting guns.

Note that these effects are produced not just by illegal or prescription drugs. Many over-the-counter medications also have considerable side effects. These may be multiplied when certain drugs are taken together or with alcohol. Read the label of any medication you take, even common non-prescription medications, or consult your physician or pharmacist for possible side effects. If the label advises against driving or operating equipment while taking the medication, you should also avoid using a firearm while taking it.

Store guns so they are inaccessible to unauthorized persons.

It is your responsibility as a gun owner to take reasonable steps to prevent unauthorized persons (especially children) from handling or otherwise having access to your firearms.

You have a number of options for accomplishing this, which are discussed in greater detail in Chapter 2: Safe Firearm Storage. The particular storage method you choose will be based upon your own particular home situation and security needs.

Be aware that certain types of guns and many shooting activities require additional safety precautions.

There are many different types of firearms, some of which require additional safety rules or procedures for proper operation. These are commonly found in your gun's owner's manual. Also, most sport shooting activities have developed sets of rules to ensure safety during competition. These rules are generally sport-specific; the procedures for loading your firearm and commencing fire, for example, are different in NRA High Power competition than in NRA Three-Gun matches (see Chapter 18: Rifle Shooting Activities).

SPECIAL RESPONSIBILITIES FOR PARENTS

Parents should be aware that a child could discover a gun when a responsible adult is not present. This situation could occur in the child's own home, the home of a neighbor, friend, or relative, or in a public place (such as a park). To avoid the possibility of an accident in such a situation, the child should be taught to apply the following gun safety rules:

If you see a gun: STOP! DON'T TOUCH. RUN AWAY. TELL A GROWN-UP.

These four rules are part of a special accident-prevention program known as the Eddie Eagle GunSafe® Program. Developed by the NRA for young children (pre-kindergarden through fourth grade), it uses the friendly character of Eddie Eagle to teach children to follow Eddie's four rules.

CHAPTER 2
Safe Firearm Storage

Safe gun storage is an integral part of gun safety, and one of your prime responsibilities as a gun owner. By storing your guns safely, you not only avoid the possibility of an accidental shooting involving a child or other untrained person; you may also prevent a criminal from using your firearm against an innocent person. In addition, some jurisdictions have laws mandating secure firearm storage, and almost all jurisdictions have criminal negligence laws that can be applied to gun owners who do not take reasonable precautions in storing their firearms. A gun owner may also be liable to a civil lawsuit in the event that his or her unsecured gun is stolen and subsequently used during the commission of a crime.

Any firearm storage method chosen must provide an adequate level of protection to prevent unauthorized persons from accessing the guns. The determination of what is "adequate protection" is a matter of judgment on the part of the gun owner, and will vary with the situation. Also, the storage method or device used must allow any gun used for home protection to be quickly retrieved to repel an intruder or an attack. Be aware that storage devices that provide a high level of security often do not allow quick firearm access. Additionally, a gun storage method should provide some level of concealment, as a gun that is not seen is less likely to be stolen.

There is no one best method of gun storage or one best type of locking or storage device. Each has advantages and limitations. You must choose the firearm storage method that is best for you, given your circumstances and preferences. It is also incumbent upon you as a responsible, law-abiding gun owner to know and observe all applicable state and local laws regarding safe gun storage.

TYPES OF LOCKING MECHANISMS

All storage methods designed to prevent unauthorized access utilize some sort of locking mechanism. Different types of locking mechanisms offer varying degrees of security and accessibility.

Keyed locks, such as padlocks and the lockable doors of closets or storage rooms, can offer a certain level of security (depending upon the construction of the lock and the door). A key-operated padlock may be used to lock a gun case closed, and some gun safes can also be operated with a key. However, under stress or in darkness it may be difficult for some to locate the correct key or to manipulate it in the lock.

Combination locks are often found on padlocks, as well as on gun safes. Such locks may range from simple triple-rotary-tumbler models to units that rival the mechanisms found on bank vaults. For many people, combination locks are both secure and familiar to use. Under stress, however, lock combinations can be forgotten by the gun owner, and the tumblers can be challenging to manipulate quickly and accurately. Also, in darkness or dim light, combination locks can be virtually impossible to operate.

Simplex® type locks provide a good combination of security and quick access. Such locks feature a number of buttons that are pushed in a specific order to open the device. With only minimal practice, these locks can be easily worked in total darkness. Locks having Simplex®-type mechanisms can be just as strong and tamper-resistant as any other.

Another advantage of a Simplex® lock is that incorrect entry blocks any further attempt to open the lock. A separate clearing code must be entered before the lock will accept the correct combination, making this lock even more resistant to unauthorized attempts to open it.

The basic Simplex®-type lock is a mechanical lock, and thus does not depend upon house current or batteries. Some locking devices combine Simplex® principles with modern electronics. Typically, such a storage device features a numeric keypad whose numbered buttons are pushed in a specific order to unlock.

A variation on this involves five *fingerpads*, ergonomically placed on the top or front of the device, which are pressed in a sequence (such as thumb, middle finger, little finger, ring finger) to open the device. Such locking mechanisms are frequently found on gun safes, and have the advantage of allowing relatively quick access to a home protection firearm, even in the dark. There usually is a provision for opening the box with a key in the event that the correct sequence is forgotten, or the electrical current that powers the unit is interrupted.

A new type of gun storage device uses biometrics to control access. The most common type of this device features a computer-controlled fingerprint reader to activate unlocking. Though this technology is promising, there are still questions regarding the long-term reliability of the reader to distinguish a fingerprint under a wide variety of circumstances.

TYPES OF STORAGE DEVICES

There are several methods for storing firearms inside and outside the home. *Gun cases* are commonly used for the transportation and storage of firearms. Soft-sided gun cases are typically of canvas, ballistic nylon or other fabric, and are closed with a zipper. They have the primary advantage of being light in weight, but don't offer much protection to the rifle. Some soft cases have zippers that can be secured with a small padlock.

Hard gun cases are most often made of synthetic material, though some more costly models are made of aluminum, or leather over a rigid frame. Some hard cases have integral keyed or combination locks; others feature hasps for small padlocks.

Gun cases can be used to transport a gun by air or other common carrier, or in a vehicle. Note that Federal law mandates that a gun transported across state lines

Soft (top) and hard gun cases

in your vehicle must be in a "locked container" (such as a gun case) when it cannot be stored in a compartment separate from the driver's compartment, and some states also have additional requirements for transporting guns within their boundaries.

In the home, gun cases serve to protect firearms from dust and moisture. However, as they are easily portable, they offer no protection from theft. Security is achieved only when the gun case is itself stored inside a gun safe or securely locked room.

Another form of storage is a *lockable gun rack or cabinet* allowing firearms (particularly long guns) to be displayed or stored openly. Although they are usually designed with some sort of locking feature, these devices offer no concealment and minimal security.

Gun safes offer the greatest level of security for your guns. Upper-end models provide walls and doors that are extremely difficult to defeat by brute force, high-security mechanical or electronic locks, and complex locking patterns that fasten the door to the frame in multiple locations with thick, hardened steel pins. Gun safest are generally too heavy and bulky for thieves to carry away easily, and almost all can be bolted to the floor or wall. Some also offer a degree of fire protection.

Gun safes are most appropriate for long-term firearm storage in the home. However, they may not be the ideal choice for the storage of a rifle used for home protection, as such a rifle may need to be quickly and quietly retrieved. Also, a gun safe provides little concealment value. Virtually anyone who sees it, such as visitors or workmen, will recognize it as a device for the storage of firearms or other valuable items, making it a target. Putting the gun safe in a closet or little-used room will help hide it from view.

Gun safe

STORING A GUN SAFELY IN THE HOME

Methods used for storing a gun in the home range from simply placing the rifle in a closet, standing it in a corner, or hanging it above the mantel, to securing it in a strong gun safe. Effective gun storage gives protection against access by unauthorized persons. Beyond that, there is no one best storage method. Proper gun storage for a person living alone in a rural area might well differ from what is needed in a city home with children around. Each gun owner must choose the proper balance of security, safety, ready access, price and other factors in the selection of firearm storage methods and devices.

PART II

RIFLE MECHANISMS AND OPERATION

CHAPTER 3
Introduction to Rifle Mechanisms

All firearms fundamentally take the form of a tube (known as the *barrel*) that is closed at one end, and into which are put a chemical propellant (*gunpowder*) and, on top of that, a snug-fitting projectile (*bullet*). When the gunpowder is ignited, hot, high pressure gas is created, which forces the projectile out of the open end of the barrel at high speed. Early firearms were *muzzle-loading*: the gunpowder and then the projectile were put into the barrel from the open or *muzzle* end of the barrel. In modern rifles however, the powder and bullet are combined into a single unit, the *metallic cartridge*, which also incorporates a pressure-sensitive component (*primer* or *priming compound*) that, when forcefully struck, ignites the powder. A more complete discussion on rifle ammunition will be presented in Chapter 9: Ammunition Fundamentals.

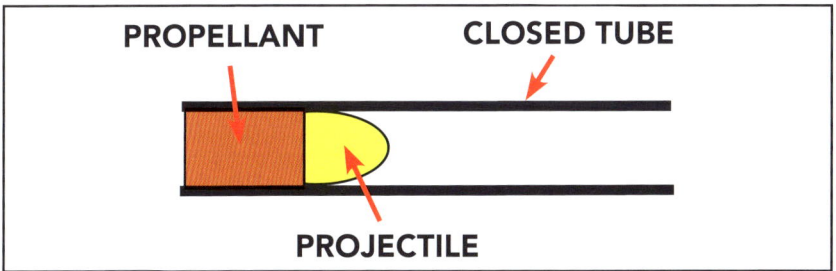

Simplified schematic of basic firearm design: a closed tube (barrel) with propellant (gunpowder) and a projectile (bullet). When the propellant is ignited, it generates high-pressure gas that forces the projectile out the open end (muzzle) at high speed.

All rifles that fire metallic cartridges are *breech-loading firearms*. A breech-loading firearm is one in which the cartridge is loaded into the rear of the barrel, or *breech*. Breech-loading firearms thus incorporate some method for both opening the breech, for cartridge loading, as well as for closing or locking the breech, to prevent the escape of the hot, high-pressure propellant gas that accelerates the bullet down the bore when the cartridge is fired.

Major components of breech-loading rifles include the *receiver*, the *barrel*, the *action* and the *stock*. The *action* determines how the gun operates, and is simply *the collection of parts that serve to fire the gun*. Action components are involved in loading a cartridge, closing and/or locking the breech, cocking the *hammer* or *firing pin* (the parts that cause the ignition of the cartridge), and extracting and/or ejecting the fired case. The *receiver* is the component in which all the action parts are housed, and to which the barrel is connected, and the *stock* allows the shooter to grip the gun and steady it against the shoulder or a rest.

RIFLE COMPONENTS

All rifles share a number of similar components, including a *trigger mechanism* that releases a spring-powered *hammer* or *firing pin* to fire the cartridge. In some action types, the firing pin is struck by the pivoting hammer, while in others, the firing pin itself is a larger, heavier part powered by a spring to set off the cartridge. In some systems of nomenclature, the spring-powered firing pin found in bolt-action rifles is called a *striker*, while the term *firing pin* is reserved for the relatively lightweight component struck by the hammer in other action types. The term "firing pin" will be used for both components in this book.

Virtually all rifle actions have one or more *safety mechanisms*. In addition, specific action types have a variety of components to close and/or lock the breech: a *bolt* in bolt-action rifles, and a *bolt* or *breech block* in semi-automatic, lever-action and

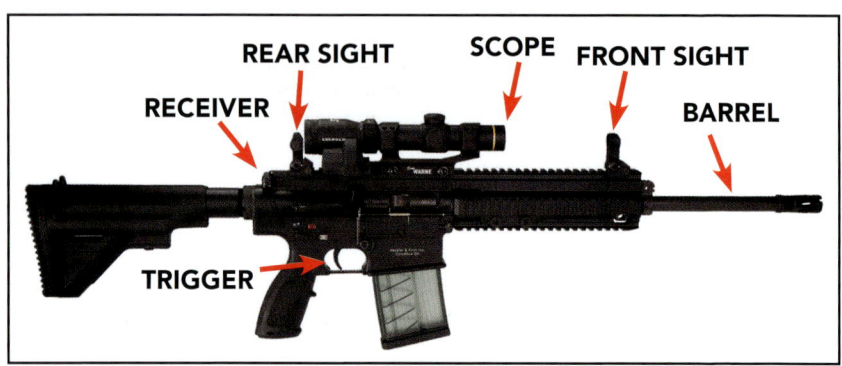

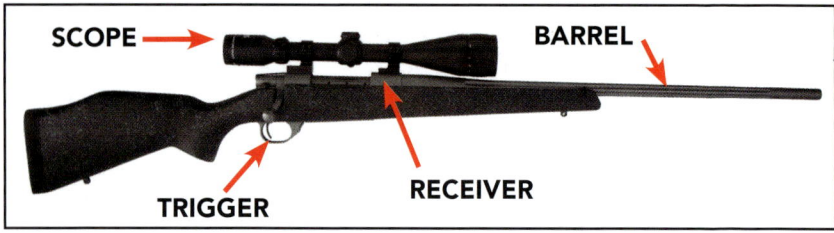

All rifles have the same major components: receiver, barrel, stock, and action parts such as the trigger, hammer, bolt and/or breech block, not all parts are visible externally.

pump-action guns. Although the difference in nomenclature is sometimes arbitrary, in general a bolt only moves forward and backwards, while a breech block also moves up and down.

Receiver— The central component of most rifles is the *receiver*, which contains the action parts, and to which are attached the stock and the barrel. Modern rifle receivers are made of steel, aluminum, titanium and even polymer materials. Some 19th-century rifles or replicas may have brass receivers.

Barrel— The *barrel* is a tube through which the bullet is propelled. In modern rifles, this is usually made of steel, and the hole through the tube, the *bore*, has spiral *rifling*, which spins the bullet for stability and accuracy. Rifling is formed by creating shallow *grooves* in the bore surface; the slightly raised areas between the grooves are called the *lands*. Occasionally, polygonal rifling is encountered. In this, instead of lands and grooves, the bore has a series of flats arranged in a hexagonal cross-section, which spirals to give the bullet spin.

At the rear of the barrel is the *chamber*, which is machined to accept a particular cartridge. The forward end of the barrel is the *muzzle*.

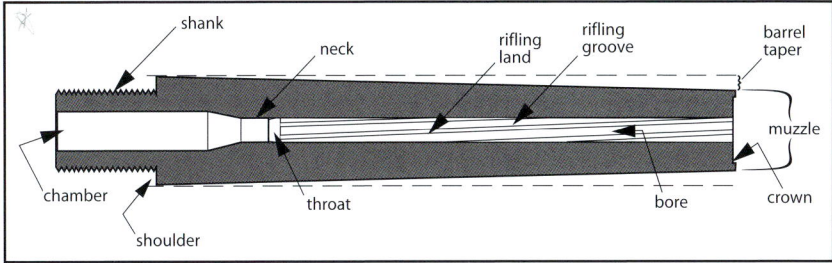

Rifling causes the bullet to spin providing projectile stability on its flight to the target.

Trigger— The *trigger* is a term used to denote both the entire mechanism that releases the hammer or firing pin to fire the cartridge, as well as the curved finger-piece that is pulled to fire the gun.

With a few older designs (and their modern replicas), the trigger directly releases the cocked hammer when it is pulled. In all other rifle types, the trigger releases the spring-loaded hammer or firing pin through an intermediary component called a *sear*. Different action types have a variety of trigger mechanisms.

Additionally, the trigger mechanisms of semi-automatic rifles contain a component called the *disconnector*, which disconnects the trigger from the sear during action cycling. The disconnector requires that the trigger be released and then pulled again for each subsequent shot, preventing full-automatic fire.

Safety Mechanisms— In general, firearm safeties can be *active* (the safety mechanism must be intentionally activated and deactivated by the shooter) or *passive* (the safety

Different types of rifles, each having its own safety and operating mechanisms

Chapter 3: Introduction to Rifle Mechanisms

mechanism functions more or less automatically). Most commonly, active safety mechanisms take the form of a lever, sliding button, etc. that can manually be moved to a "safe" position to prevent firing, and a "fire" position to allow the gun to be discharged.

Passive safeties on rifles most commonly take the form of a design feature that prevents the hammer from hitting the firing pin, or the firing pin from hitting the cartridge, unless the action is fully closed and locked. The functioning of these internal mechanisms is not apparent to the user.

Some external-hammer rifles, such as classic lever actions, usually have a half-cock notch on the hammer. This is designed to prevent the hammer from slipping off the thumb during cocking or decocking, and falling fully forward to fire a cartridge in the chamber.

Remember, safeties are mechanical devices and can fail. Always follow the Fundamental Rules for Safe Gun Handling.

Breech Closing/Locking Mechanisms— In all rifle actions, the breech is closed through the action of a *bolt* (also called a breech bolt) or a *breech block*. A bolt moves rearward to open the action and forward to close it, and locking is normally accomplished by rotation of the bolt so that protruding lugs on its head or body engage recesses in the receiver or barrel. There are exceptions to this; in some lever-action rifles, the bolt is locked by a rising wedge-shaped locking block. Moreover, in some semi-automatics firing low-pressure rimfire ammunition, the breech is not locked at all, but is kept closed by the pressure of the recoil spring and the inertia of the bolt.

A breech block may also run forward and rearward in the receiver, but usually rises or falls in some manner as to engage a locking recess in the receiver. As stated previously, consistency in this nomenclature is lacking.

TYPES OF RIFLE ACTIONS

The great majority of rifles that will be purchased for hunting, plinking, home protection or target work will be of bolt-action, semi-automatic, lever-action or pump-action design. Each of these will be discussed in detail in Chapters 4-7. Other types of rifle actions may also be encountered, including the *falling block*, *rolling block*, *trapdoor*, and *break-action*. These will be briefly covered in Chapter 8.

FIREARM CYCLE OF OPERATION

Bolt action

lever action

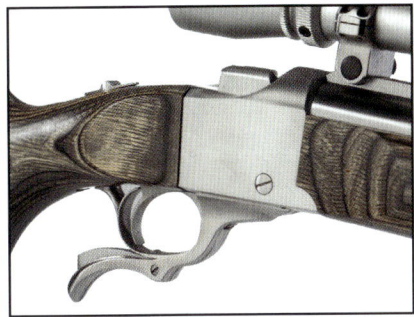
falling block

semi-auto action

pump action

hinge or break action

Regardless of design, every firearm action must allow a strict sequence of events to take place. This sequence, known as the *cycle of operation,* consists of the following steps:

Firing: occurs when the trigger is pulled and the hammer or striker is released to fly forward, causing the firing pin to hit the primer

Unlocking: the initial step in the opening of the action. In locked-breech guns, this occurs when the bolt or breech block is unlocked from the barrel or receiver. In non-locked-breech guns, such as some semi-automatic rifles (see Chapter 5: Semi-Automatic Rifle Parts and Operation), the action is kept closed simply by the recoil spring, and opens only when chamber pressure overcomes bolt inertia and spring pressure.

Extraction: the pulling of the spent cartridge case rearward out of the chamber, usually by a part called an *extractor*

Ejection: the forcible throwing of the spent case clear of the action by a component called the *ejector*

Cocking: the movement of the hammer or firing pin to its rearward position, where it is retained against spring pressure by the trigger mechanism

Feeding: the insertion of a live cartridge into the chamber by closing the bolt or breech block

Locking: the closing of the action (and, in locked-breech firearms, the engagement of the locking mechanism) so that the breech is sealed. After the *Locking* step, the cycle returns to the *Firing* step.

The sequence of the steps in the above generic cycle of operation may vary for different action types.

CHAPTER 4
Bolt-Action Rifle Parts and Operation

Bolt-action firearms consist of a *receiver*, a *bolt* which can freely move in the fore-and-aft direction inside the receiver, a *barrel* attached to the forward end of the receiver, a *magazine*, (unless it is a single shot,) a *stock*, and a *trigger mechanism*. The bolt has *lugs*, or projections, which engage recesses in the receiver or, much less commonly, the barrel or a barrel extension, to lock the action. Many turnbolt actions feature a bolt with two large forward lugs, but successful designs have been produced with three to as many as nine lugs in the *head* (front section) of the bolt. A few designs have lugs in the rear of the bolt.

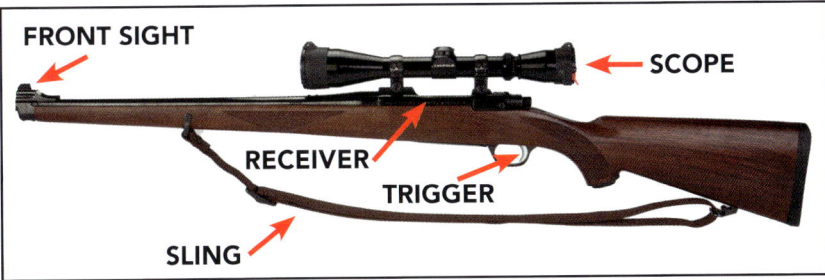

Typical bolt-action rifle, left side

The bolt also houses the *firing pin* and claw *extractor*. Ejection is often by means of a spring-loaded plunger in the bolt face, or, alternatively, by a fixed blade or finger mounted in the receiver. At the rear of the bolt is the *bolt shroud*, which houses the *cocking piece* at the rear of the firing pin.

An *ejection port* (also called *loading port* in some guns) in the receiver provides a means for fired cartridge cases to exit the action, or, at times, to load a fresh cartridge directly into the chamber. Ignition is by way of a spring-loaded firing pin.

BOLT-ACTION OPERATING PRINCIPLES

In the vast majority of bolt-action rifles, the bolt has a rigid handle that projects laterally, and which is lifted to turn the bolt. This does two things. First, lifting the bolt handle rotates the bolt anywhere from around 60 to 90 degrees, which unlocks the bolt lugs from their locking recesses, and begins the process of extracting the case from the chamber. This extraction is aided by an *extraction cam* on the rear of the receiver, which engages the root of the bolt handle when the handle is lifted. This cam provides significant leverage to pull a tight case free of the chamber.

Second, on virtually all modern bolt-action rifles, lifting the bolt handle also cocks the firing pin. Rifles of this design are thus called *cock on opening*. Some older military rifle designs cock the firing pin on bolt downturn; these are called *cock on closing* actions.

Above, typical bolt-action rifle.
Right, the bolt removed from the rifle

Close-up of the bolt head.

A very few older bolt-action rifles intended for younger shooters have a large knob on the end of the bolt which must be forcibly retracted to cock the firing pin. Requiring the shooter to cock the firing pin in a separate operation from working the bolt was thought to provide an extra measure of safety.

Firing pin cocking is accomplished by a helical cam on the rear face of the bolt body, which contacts the *cocking piece* at the end of the firing pin. Bolt rotation produced when the handle is lifted causes the cam to pull the cocking piece and firing pin rearward against spring tension. At full cock, the cocking piece is held rearward by the trigger mechanism, and is retained in this cocked position when the bolt is closed.

With the bolt handle lifted, the bolt can be pulled rearward manually, fully extracting and ejecting the spent case. Bolt-action extractors may take a number of forms, but all are basically claws mounted in the bolt head that grip the case rim. Ejection is often provided by a spring-loaded plunger in the bolt face that spins the case out of the action. Alternatively, ejection may be provided by a receiver-mounted blade that runs in a groove in the bolt, and which hits the case when the bolt is pulled rearward.

The bolt is pulled all the way to the rear, where it will contact the *bolt stop*. This component prevents the bolt from being pulled all the way out of the gun. (The bolt stop can be disengaged to allow bolt removal for cleaning.) With a single-shot bolt-action rifle, the shooter then puts a cartridge into the gun through the loading port. The bolt is then pushed forward to feed the cartridge into the chamber, and rotated to lock.

With repeater rifles, as the bolt goes forward, the edge of the forward-moving bolt face catches the rim of the top cartridge in the magazine, pushing it forward out of the magazine and into the chamber. Some bolts, such as the original Mauser 98, the pre-1964 Winchester 70 and Ruger 77, have a large claw extractor attached to the outside of the bolt, designed so that the case rim slides under the claw as the cartridge exits the magazine. The cartridge is then controlled by the extractor. These *controlled round feed* designs allow easy extraction of an unfired cartridge. Such designs also prevent double feeding (a situation in which faulty or indecisive bolt manipulation causes two cartridges to be released from the magazine and jam in the action). For this latter reason, controlled round feed rifles are often preferred for hunting dangerous game.

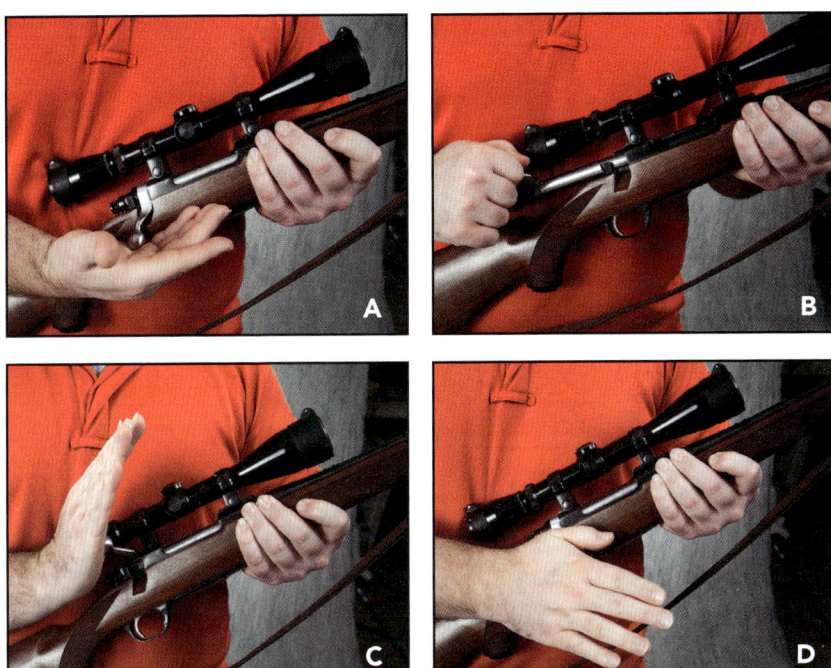

Cycling the bolt action: lift the bolt (A), slide the bolt fully to the rear (B), slide bolt fully forward (C), push bolt handle down (D).

Other bolt-action designs employ a claw in the bolt head that snaps over the case rim when the cartridge fully enters the chamber. Such designs are called *push feed designs*, as the cartridge is pushed into the chamber by the bolt, but not controlled.

When the bolt is fully forward, the handle is rotated downward to lock the action. Cam surfaces inside the receiver serve to pull the bolt head forward slightly as the bolt handle is turned down. The leverage provided by these cams serves to positively chamber a cartridge even if it is slightly bulged or contaminated with dust or dirt.

Finally, the rifle may be fired by pulling the trigger. This will release the cocked firing pin to fly forward to hit the primer and ignite the powder in the case.

BOLT-ACTION RIFLE MAGAZINES

Bolt-action rifles may have *internal* or *detachable box magazines*, the latter dropped from the gun by a *magazine* catch or *magazine release*.

Box magazines typically have a steel, aluminum or plastic *body* which houses the cartridges and the magazine's internal components. At the bottom of the magazine is a *floorplate*, usually of the same material. This is often removable to allow magazine cleaning. Inside the magazine are the *magazine spring* and *follower*, which together push the cartridges in the magazine upward into position for reliable feeding.

The internal box magazines found in some bolt-action rifles are similar in design principles to external box magazines, and feature a box which encloses the cartridges,

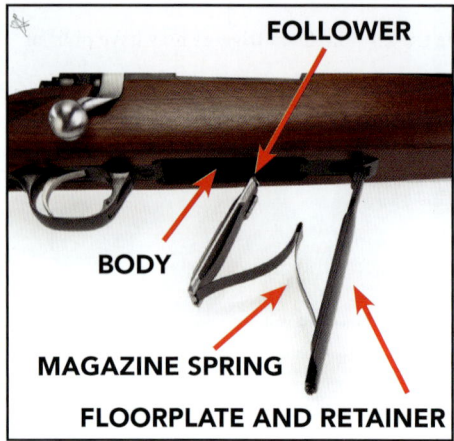

This rifle magazine consists of a magazine spring, follower, magazine body, floorplate and floorplate retainer. Some magazines have a welded floorplate.

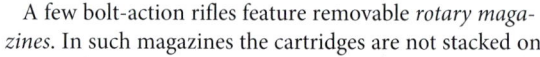

Stripper clips

a follower, and a magazine spring. Many rifles with internal magazines have a hinged *floorplate* attached to the rifle's *bottom metal,* the aluminum or steel component on the underside of the stock that comprises the magazine opening, trigger guard and stock screw seats. When the *floorplate latch* is released, the floorplate swings down and drops all the cartridges in the magazine to unload the rifle. An internal magazine lacking a floorplate is said to be a *blind* magazine.

Bolt-action rifles with internal magazines must be loaded by inserting cartridges into the magazine through the ejection port. To speed this process, some rifles intended for target or military use are loaded through the open action by means of *stripper clips*, metal clips which grip the rims of a number of cartridges. When a loaded stripper clip is properly positioned in the receiver, above the magazine, the cartridges may be slid downward off the clip and into the magazine, quickly loading the rifle.

A few bolt-action rifles feature removable *rotary magazines*. In such magazines the cartridges are not stacked on top of each other as in box magazines, but are positioned radially inside the magazine, rather like the cartridges in a revolver cylinder. Some rimfire bolt-action rifles have a tubular magazine located under the barrel. These magazines are loaded by way of an opening in the forward end of the tube.

BOLT-ACTION TRIGGER MECHANISMS

A bolt-action rifle with a removable magazine

Bolt action rifles achieve ignition by way of a spring-powered firing pin inside the bolt that is held to the rear by the trigger mechanisms. Some older military rifles feature *direct-pull triggers,* in which the trigger directly engages the cocking piece. More common in modern rifles are *override triggers,* in which a separate pivoting *sear* holds the cocking piece rearward, supported at its free end by the trigger. When the trigger is pulled, the sear is forced to pivot downward as the spring-powered firing pin overrides it. Because of the inherent leverage benefits of such designs, override triggers are capable of producing a lighter and crisper trigger pull than direct-pull triggers. Bolt-action rifle triggers may be of single-stage or two-stage design; the former type is most frequently encountered.

Some target rifles have *three-* or *four-lever triggers*. In these designs, adding more leverage points permits a lighter but still reliable trigger pull. Such triggers may have pulls of less than one ounce.

Additionally, many bolt-action triggers allow easy adjustment of the pull weight, *overtravel* (trigger movement after the sear is released) and, sometimes, sear engagement with the trigger piece. Such adjustments are usually best left to a gunsmith, as an improperly-adjusted trigger can be unreliable and unsafe.

BOLT-ACTION SAFETY MECHANISMS

Active safety mechanisms on bolt action rifles take the form of a safety lever attached to the trigger unit that blocks the trigger or sear, or a pivoting lever attached to the bolt shroud that, when engaged, prevents forward movement of the firing pin.

Safety mechanisms can be of *two-position* or *three-position* design. Two-position safeties can be put in either the "fire" or "safe" positions. In many of these, the bolt can be worked to remove cartridges from the magazine with the safety on. Three-position safeties also allow "fire" and "safe" positions, but additionally have a second "safe" position in which the bolt is locked.

Passive safety systems include design features that prevent the firing pin from hitting the cartridge primer unless the bolt handle is turned down, and an easily-visible cocking piece that protrudes from the rear of the bolt shroud when the rifle is cocked.

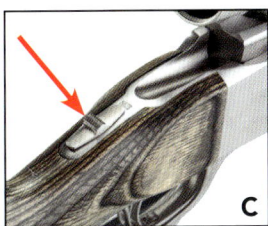

Different types of bolt-action rifle safeties: pivoting wing on bolt shroud (A), receiver-mounted lever (B) and tang-mounted sliding button (C).

BOLT ACTION CYCLE OF OPERATION

All bolt-action rifles have essentially the same cycle of operation. However, some steps in the cycle may not apply to all action types.

Firing— Pulling the trigger releases the firing pin, causing the primer to be struck and the cartridge to be fired.

Unlocking— Lifting the bolt handle disengages the locking lugs from their recesses in the receiver or barrel, unlocking the action.

Extraction— Initial extraction is provided by the extraction cam on the receiver; further retraction of the bolt completes case extraction from the chamber.

Ejection— As the bolt moves to the rear with the spent cartridge case, an ejector—usually a plunger in the bolt face or a standing blade mounted in the receiver—pushes against the case head, throwing the case out of the action through the ejection port.

Chapter 4: Bolt-Action Rifle Parts and Operation

Cocking— With cock-on-opening actions, cocking of the firing pin is achieved on bolt lift. With cock-on-closing actions, bolt turn-down cocks the firing pin. In both cases, the cocked firing pin is held rearward by the sear.

Feeding— With repeater rifles, moving the bolt forward strips a cartridge from the magazine and feeds it into the chamber. With single shot rifles, a cartridge must first be manually placed into the action through the loading port, and the bolt returned forward to feed the cartridge into the chamber.

Locking— Locking of the action is accomplished by turning the bolt handle completely downward.

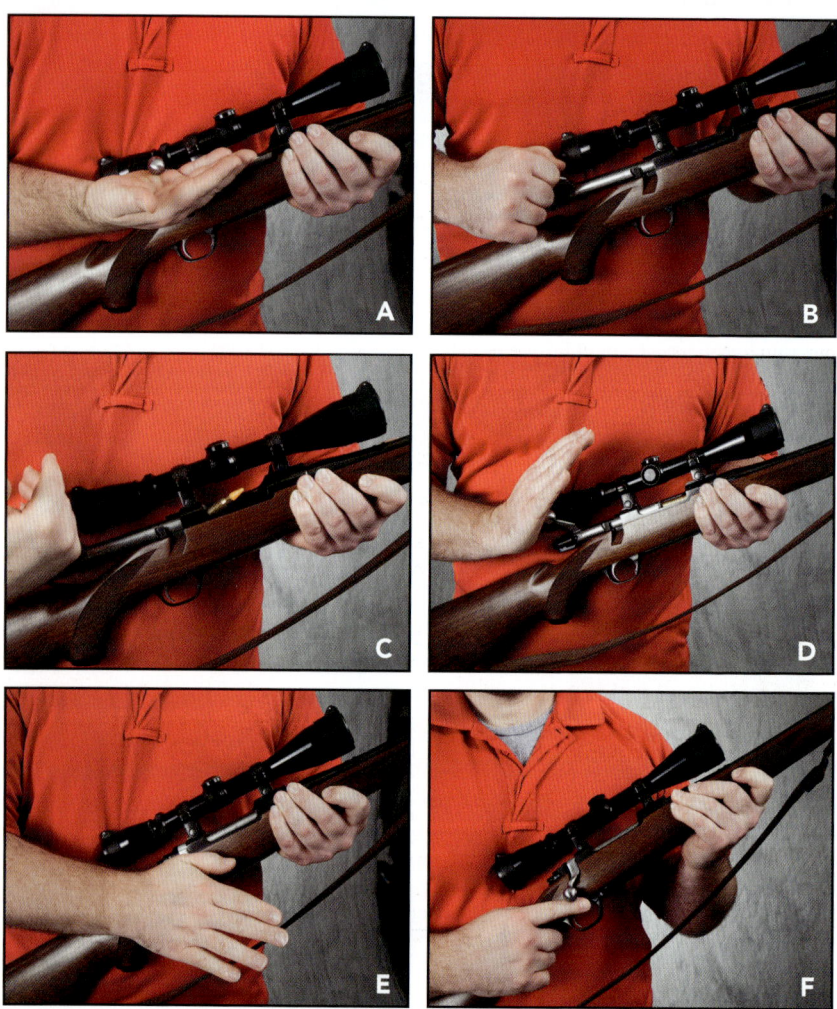

Bolt-action rifle cycle of operation. Bolt handle is lifted to cock the firing pin and unlock the action (A), and bolt is retracted rearward to extract (B), and eject chambered cartridge (fired or unfired) (C). Bolt is pushed forward to strip fresh cartridge from magazine, and feed it into chamber (D). Bolt handle is turned down to lock action (E). The cartridge is now chambered and the bolt is locked in place (F).

OPERATING BOLT-ACTION RIFLES

Operating bolt-action rifles consists of the procedures to safely and efficiently load, fire, and unload these guns.

LOADING

Loading means filling an empty gun with cartridges. Different procedures are required for rifles having detachable magazines, rifles having non-detachable magazines, and single-shot rifles.

LOADING A DETACHABLE BOLT-ACTION RIFLE MAGAZINE

In guns having detachable magazines, this process involves, first, loading the empty magazine and then inserting the magazine into the gun and feeding a live cartridge into the chamber.

The empty magazine should be grasped by the fingers of the support or non-firing hand (the hand that is not used to pull the trigger), with the top of the magazine facing upward and the front of the magazine oriented toward the firing hand. The firing hand picks up a live cartridge and brings it to the top of the magazine, with the case head facing the magazine and the bullet pointing away from the magazine. The case rim is used to depress the magazine follower slightly, and the cartridge is then slid under the feed lips of the magazine all the way to the rear. The case rim of the next cartridge to be loaded depresses the top cartridge in the magazine, and itself is slid under the magazine feed lips. This process is repeated for each cartridge until the magazine is fully loaded. Finally, the shooter should slap the rear of the loaded magazine sharply against the palm of the hand or other object, to ensure that all cartridges are positioned to the rear of the magazine for proper feeding.

  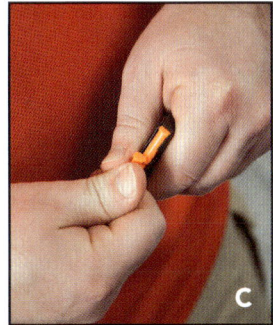

Loading detachable bolt-action rifle magazines: Empty magazine with live cartridge in hand (A), continue adding live cartridges to magazine (B), repeat until magazine is full (C).

Chapter 4: Bolt-Action Rifle Parts and Operation

LOADING BOLT-ACTION RIFLES

Loading a Rifle with a Detachable Magazine.

Grasp the rifle magazine with the firing hand (the hand used to pull the trigger), while your non-firing hand grips the rifle fore-end. Keeping the rifle pointing in a safe direction, use your firing hand to bring the magazine to the magazine well under the receiver of the gun, and insert the magazine fully. The magazine must be inserted in the proper orientation, with the bullets facing forward. Normally, a click is heard when the magazine is fully seated. You may also need to slap the floorplate or basepad to ensure proper seating.

Loading a detachable magazine into a bolt-action rifle

Loading a Rifle with a Non-Detachable Magazine

Bolt-action rifles having non-detachable magazines must be loaded through the ejection port of the receiver. With the bolt fully retracted, and the rifle held in the left hand (for a right-handed rifle), individually insert cartridges into the receiver through the ejection port, push each one downward against the magazine follower. The follower will be

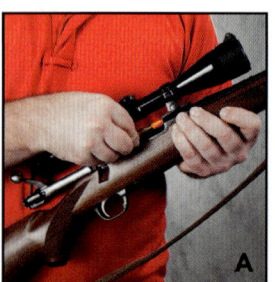 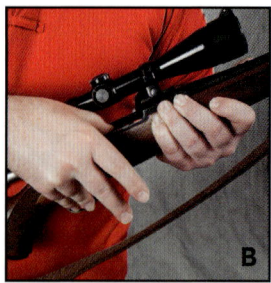 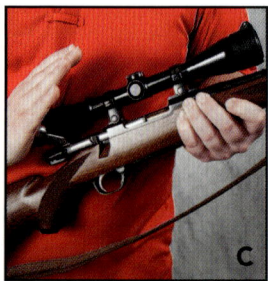

Loading a bolt-action rifle with a non-detachable magazine: With the action open (A), push a live cartridge into magazine (B), repeat until magazine full, then close action (C).

depressed and each cartridge should slip under the magazine feed lips with an audible click. When no more cartridges can be inserted into the magazine in this way, loading is complete.

Loading a Single-Shot Bolt-Action Rifle

With the bolt fully retracted, insert a fresh cartridge into the receiver through the ejection port, bullet facing forward. The cartridge will rest on the floor of the receiver.

Loading a Cartridge into the Chamber

Grip the rifle stock with the support hand and use the firing hand to push the bolt fully

 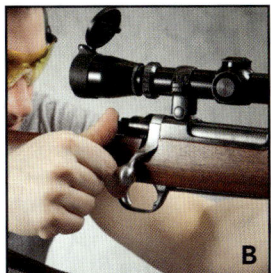 

Firing a bolt-action rifle: With a loaded rifle, safety on, align the site with the target (A), disengage the safety (B), apply increasing pressure to the trigger until the rifle fires (C).

forward, chambering a loaded cartridge. Turn the bolt handle down fully to lock the action.

Once a cartridge has been chambered, the shooter may commence firing. If there is to be a delay in firing, the rifle should be made safe by either engaging the safety or, if firing is to be postponed for a considerable period of time, unloading the rifle.

FIRING

Firing the loaded bolt-action rifle involves, first, assuming the desired shooting position, and mounting the gun against the shoulder. With the trigger finger outside the trigger guard, the rifle is then taken from the "safe" condition to the "fire" condition.

The rifle is then aligned with the target. At this time, the trigger finger may enter the trigger guard and contact the trigger, and the sequence of events that culminate in firing a shot can begin.

Upon firing the first shot, the shooter may continue to fire a number of shots or may elect to stop shooting. Alternatively, the shooter may put the loaded rifle on the shooting bench. If the gun is simply lowered, and another shot is to be immediately fired, there is no need to engage the safety. On the other hand, a loaded rifle placed on a bench should, at the very least, have its safety put into the "safe" condition. Also, if the rifle is put on the shooting bench and the shooter intends to walk away from it for any reason, even for a moment, the rifle should be fully unloaded and left on the bench with the action open and the magazine removed.

UNLOADING

Unloading a Bolt-Action Rifle with a Detachable Magazine

To unload a bolt-action rifle with a detachable magazine, first ensure that the gun is pointed in a safe direction, and engage the safety. Remove the trigger finger from the trigger and place it outside the trigger guard, alongside the frame. Next, press the magazine release button to drop the magazine from the gun. This may be located in a variety of positions--most often just forward of the trigger guard, or, occasionally, on the side of the stock.

Once the magazine is removed from the rifle, it is still necessary to extract the live cartridge from the chamber. With the rifle still pointed in a safe direction, use the firing hand to lift and retract the bolt handle fully to the rear. This will extract the live cartridge

 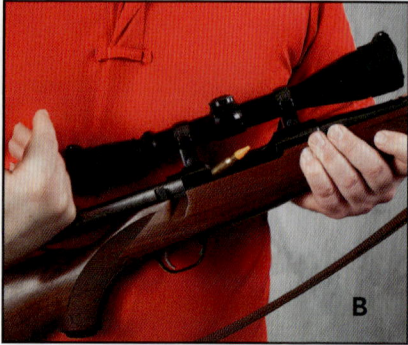

Unloading a bolt-action rifle. Two ways to unload: open floorplate and cycle the action (A), cycle the action until the magazine is empty (B).

from the chamber and eject it. At this time, with the bolt fully rearward, visually and physically inspect the chamber to ensure the rifle is unloaded.

Rifles that will not allow the bolt to be cycled with the safety on will have to be put in the "fire" condition to remove the live cartridge from the chamber. With such guns, it is even more important for the rifle to be kept pointing in a safe direction during unloading.

Unloading a Bolt-Action Rifle with a Non-Detachable Magazine

Bolt-action rifles having non-detachable magazines may be unloaded in two ways. On guns with hinged floorplates, the floorplate latch is engaged to open the floorplate, causing the cartridges in the magazine to be dumped out. Then, with the safety on and the rifle pointed in a safe direction, the bolt can be lifted and retracted to extract and eject the live cartridge in the chamber.

With bolt-action rifles lacking floorplates, the safety should be engaged, the rifle pointed in a safe direction, and the bolt cycled repeatedly to work all the cartridges in the magazine out of the gun. Visually and physically inspect the chamber and magazine well to ensure the rifle is unloaded. In addition, although this will work with a tubular-magazine, in some models unloading can be accomplished by removing the inner magazine tube and then retracting the bolt handle to eject any cartridge that may be in the chamber.

Unloading a Single-Shot Bolt-Action Rifle

Engage the rifle's safety, and lift and retract the bolt to extract the live cartridge from the chamber. Visually and physically inspect the chamber to ensure the rifle is unloaded.

CHAPTER 5
Semi-Automatic Rifle Parts and Operation

In general, semi-automatic firearms utilize the pressure from the gas generated by the ignition of the cartridge to perform the cycle of operation.

Semi-automatic rifles fundamentally consist of a *receiver*, a *bolt* which can freely move in the fore-and-aft direction inside the receiver, a *barrel* attached to the forward end of the receiver, a *magazine*, a *stock*, and a *trigger mechanism*. A *recoil spring* slows the opening of the action, absorbs some of the recoil force generated upon firing, and pushes the bolt forward to close the action.

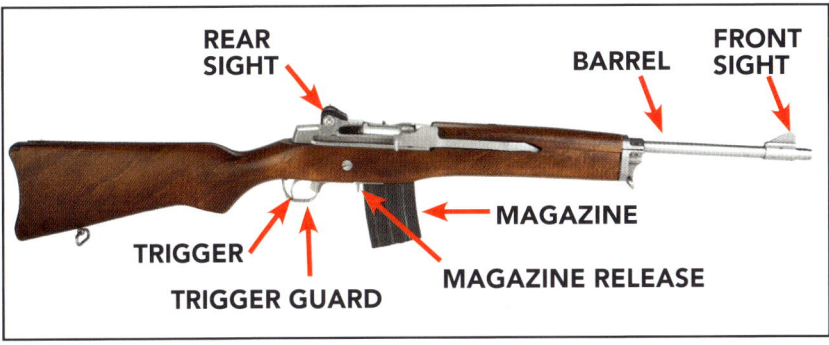

Typical semi-automatic rifle (right side) with major parts indicated

Note that some semi-automatic rifles, such as the AR-15, have both an *upper* and *lower receiver*.

Semi-automatic rifles chambered for rimfire cartridges may be of blowback design, in which the inertia of the bolt and the pressure of the recoil spring alone serve to close the action. Centerfire cartridges almost always work at much higher pressures, however, and require locked-breech semi-automatic actions. In these, the bolt locks the action closed usually through one or more protruding *lugs* on the bolt that engage corresponding recesses in the barrel or receiver.

The bolt also houses the *firing pin* and claw *extractor*. Ejection is often by means of a spring-loaded plunger in the bolt face, or, alternatively, by a fixed blade or finger mounted in the receiver. An *ejection port* in the receiver provides a means for fired cartridge cases to exit the action, or, at times, to load a fresh cartridge directly into the chamber. Ignition is by either an internal hammer or a spring-loaded firing pin.

Semi-automatic rifles utilizing detachable magazines also feature a *magazine* catch or *magazine release*. This is a button or latch that, when depressed, releases the magazine from the gun.

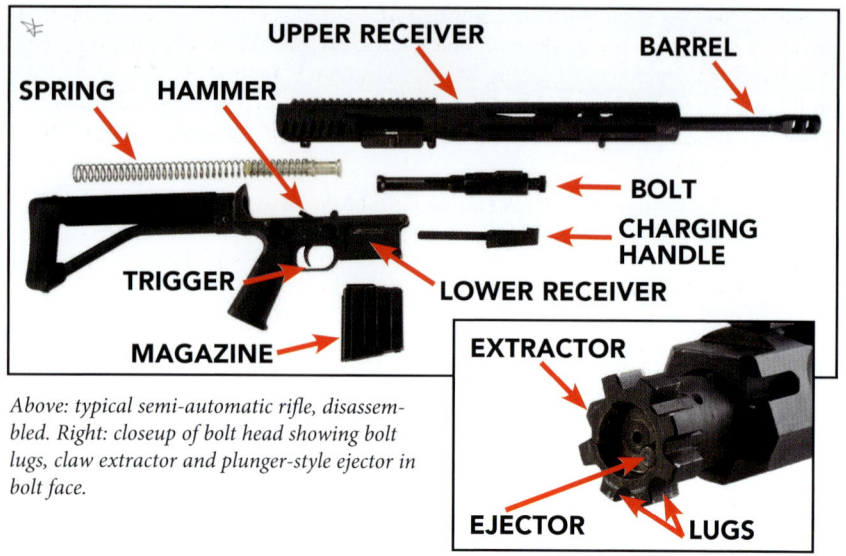

Above: typical semi-automatic rifle, disassembled. Right: closeup of bolt head showing bolt lugs, claw extractor and plunger-style ejector in bolt face.

TYPES OF SEMI-AUTOMATIC RIFLE MECHANISMS

The vast majority of semi-automatic rifles have either *blowback-operated* or *gas-operated* actions.

BLOWBACK-OPERATED ACTIONS

In *blowback-operated* semi-automatic rifles, the action is not mechanically locked, and the weight of a heavy bolt, plus a strong recoil spring, is all that keeps the action closed. Upon firing, chamber pressure created by cartridge ignition pushes the bolt rearward, compressing the recoil spring. The inertia of the bolt, aided by spring resistance, keeps the action closed long enough for the bullet to exit the muzzle and pressure in the chamber and bore to drop to a safe level. Blowback designs are generally restricted to rifles firing low-powered .17- and .22-caliber rimfire cartridges.

A few semi-automatic rifles have been made with delayed blowback actions. In these the action is not locked, but a mechanical device retards rearward movement of the bolt just long enough for gas pressure to drop to safe levels in the chamber and bore. Delayed-blowback actions have been used successfully with modern high-pressure centerfire cartridges.

GAS-OPERATED ACTIONS

In gas-operated actions, high-pressure propellant gas is bled from the bore through a small hole in the barrel. This, in turn, most commonly exerts pressure on a *gas piston*. The gas piston is connected to an operating rod (also called, in different designs, an *action bar* or *piston extension*) that engages either the bolt or a *bolt carrier* in which the bolt is mounted. In many designs, rearward movement of the operating rod causes camming surfaces on the bolt carrier to rotate the bolt, taking the bolt lugs out of engagement with their locking recesses in the barrel or receiver. In some other designs, the operating rod causes the bolt to be cammed downward or upward out of a locking recess in the receiver. In both types, once the bolt is unlocked from the barrel or receiver, the bolt and carrier continue rearward to extract and eject the empty shell, cock the hammer or firing pin, and compress the recoil spring. At the end of rearward travel, the compressed recoil spring impels the bolt and carrier forward, feeding a new cartridge into the chamber and closing and locking the action.

Another type is the *direct impingement* semi-automatic actions, such as the AR-15/M16 design. In these, the high-pressure gas bled from the bore goes down a gas tube to push directly on the bolt carrier. As the bolt carrier moves rearward under this pressure, cams force the bolt head to turn, unlocking its lugs from the barrel extension. Further rearward motion causes the empty cartridge case to be extracted and ejected, the hammer to be cocked and the recoil spring to be compressed. As with gas piston designs, the compressed recoil spring causes the bolt and carrier to go forward, stripping a fresh cartridge from the magazine and feeding it into the chamber, and finally closing and locking the action.

SEMI-AUTOMATIC RIFLE MAGAZINES

Most semi-automatic firearms utilize detachable *box magazines.*

Box magazines typically have a steel, aluminum or plastic *body* which houses the cartridges and the magazine's internal components. At the bottom of the magazine is a *floorplate*, usually of the same material. This is often removable to allow magazine cleaning. Inside the magazine are the *magazine spring* and *follower*, which together push the cartridges in the magazine upward into position for reliable feeding.

A few semi-automatic rifles, usually older military designs, have a non-detachable internal box magazine. Depending upon the particular gun model, such magazines are loaded in a variety of ways, often by means of a *clip*, a device, usually of metal, that holds a number of cartridges together as a unit, and which allows the cartridges to be loaded into the gun's magazine. In some designs, such magazines are loaded by means of *stripper clips*, metal clips which grip the rims of a number of cartridges. When a loaded stripper clip is properly positioned in the receiver, above the magazine, the cartridges may be slid downward off the clip and into the magazine, loading the rifle.

The M1 Garand, in contrast, utilizes an *en bloc* clip, which is inserted with the cartridges into the gun's magazine. When all the cartridges have been fired, the clip is ejected from the action.

This rifle magazine consists of a magazine spring, follower, magazine body, floorplate and floorplate retainer. Some magazines have a welded floorplate.

Chapter 5: Semi-Automatic Rifle Parts and Operation

(Left) Stripper clip and (right) en bloc clip

Some older .22 rimfire semi-automatic rifles will be encountered with *tubular magazines*. These are most often located beneath the barrel, but occasionally are located in the buttstock. These magazines are loaded by way of an opening in the forward end of the tube, or an opening in the buttstock. A few semi-automatic rifles also feature

Loading a tubular magazine

removable *rotary magazines*. In such magazines the cartridges are not stacked on top of each other as in box magazines, but are positioned radially inside the magazine, rather like the cartridges in a revolver cylinder.

SEMI-AUTOMATIC TRIGGER MECHANISMS

Modern semi-automatic rifles can achieve ignition by way of either an internal hammer, or by a spring-powered firing pin that is held to the rear by the sear. Semi-automatic rifles also incorporate some sort of *disconnector* mechanism, which requires that the trigger be pulled each time a shot is fired.

As with bolt-action rifles, triggers for semi-automatic rifles may be of single-stage or two-stage design. Most military-style rifles have two-stage triggers. Semi-autos for target use may have either single- or two-stage triggers, with light, crisp trigger pulls.

SEMI-AUTOMATIC SAFETY MECHANISMS

Semi-automatic rifle safety systems may take a number of forms: a crossbolt safety mounted at the front or rear of the trigger guard, a lever in front of the trigger guard, or a pivoting lever located on one or both sides of the receiver. Semi-automatic safeties typically block the trigger or sear.

Most semi-automatic rifles also incorporate a number of passive safety features. Most common are designs that prevent the hammer from contacting the firing pin unless the action is fully closed and locked.

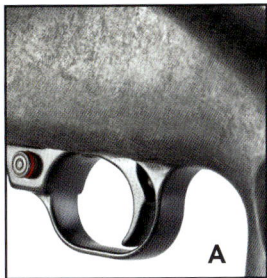 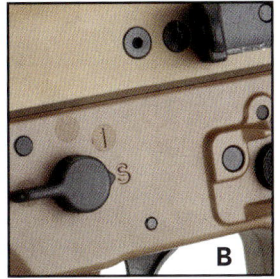 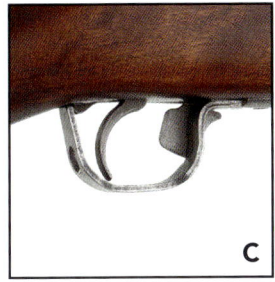

Different types of semi-automatic rifle safeties: crossbolt (A), pivoting receiver-mounted lever (B), and lever forward of the trigger guard (C).

SEMI-AUTOMATIC CYCLE OF OPERATION

All semi-automatic rifles have essentially the same cycle of operation. However, some steps in the cycle may not apply to all action types.

Firing— Pulling the trigger releases an internal hammer or firing pin, causing the primer to be struck and the cartridge to be fired.

Unlocking— The mechanics of unlocking is determined by the nature of the semi-automatic mechanism. Blowback-operated systems are by definition unlocked, so no unlocking is necessary. In such systems, the action opens simply when the gas pressure in the chamber and bore overcomes the forward force of the recoil spring and the inertia of the slide or bolt. In gas-operated actions, gas pressure tapped from the bore pushes the bolt carrier rearward, either directly or through an operating rod system, causing the bolt to unlock from the receiver or barrel.

Extraction— A claw extractor mounted on the bolt engages the rim of the cartridge case and pulls the case from the chamber after the action unlocks.

Ejection— As the bolt moves to the rear carrying a spent cartridge case, an ejector—usually a plunger in the bolt face or a standing blade mounted in the receiver—contacts the case head, throwing the case out of the action through the ejection port.

Cocking— At or near the extreme rearward limit of its travel, the reciprocating bolt (or bolt carrier) cocks the hammer or firing pin, which is held rearward against spring tension by the trigger mechanism.

Feeding— The compressed recoil spring pushes the slide rapidly forward, stripping a cartridge from the magazine and feeding it into the chamber.

Locking— With locked-breech semiautomatic designs, locking of the action occurs during the last fraction of an inch of forward motion of the bolt and carrier. In some designs, the bolt rotates to bring its locking lugs into contact with engagement surfaces in the barrel. In other designs, the forward movement of the carrier cams the bolt up or down into a locking recess in the receiver. With blowback-operated designs, no locking occurs; the momentum of the forward-moving bolt is sufficient to fully chamber a cartridge and close the action (at which point the action is said to be *in battery*). Only the force of the compressed recoil spring, combined with the inertia of the bolt, keeps the action closed.

Chapter 5: Semi-Automatic Rifle Parts and Operation

OPERATING SEMI-AUTOMATIC RIFLES

Operating semi-automatic rifles consists of the procedures to safely and efficiently load, fire, and unload these guns.

LOADING

Loading means filling an empty gun with cartridges. This process involves, first, loading the empty magazine and then (with a detachable magazine) inserting the magazine into the gun and feeding a live cartridge into the chamber.

LOADING THE SEMI-AUTOMATIC RIFLE MAGAZINE

The magazine should be grasped by the fingers of the support (non-firing) hand, with the top of the magazine facing upward and the front of the magazine oriented toward the firing hand. The firing hand picks up a live cartridge and brings it to the top of the magazine, with the case head facing the magazine and the bullet pointing away from the magazine. The case rim is used to depress the magazine follower slightly, and the cartridge is then slid under the feed lips of the magazine all the way to the rear. The case rim of the next cartridge to be loaded depresses the top cartridge in the magazine, and itself is slid under the magazine feed lips. This process is repeated for each cartridge until the magazine is loaded. Finally, the shooter should slap the rear of the loaded magazine sharply with the hand or other object, to ensure that all cartridges are positioned to the rear of the unit, for proper feeding.

Loading semi-automatic rifle magazines: With an empty magazine load a live cartridges into the magazine (A), pushing the cartridge down below the feed lips (B), continue loading until the magazine is full (C).

LOADING SEMI-AUTOMATIC RIFLES

Loading a Rifle with a Detachable Magazine

The rifle is grasped with the firing hand, with the trigger finger outside the trigger guard, alongside the stock. With the rifle pointing in a safe direction, the support hand brings the magazine to the magazine well under the receiver of the gun, and inserts the magazine fully. The magazine must be inserted in the proper orientation, with the bullets facing forward. Normally, a click is heard when the magazine is fully seated. The shooter may also slap the floorplate or basepad to ensure proper seating.

 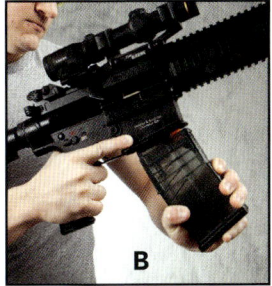 

Loading a detachable magazine into a semi-automatic rifle: With a loaded magazine, cartridge facing forward (A), insert into the magazine well (B) then slap the bottom of magazine to ensure it is fully seated (C).

Loading a Rifle with a Non-Detachable Magazine

Tubular magazines used in semi-automatic rifles can be located under the barrel or in the buttstock. Virtually all such guns are chambered for .22 rimfire ammunition, and loading is accomplished in a number of ways. In some designs, cartridges are loaded through a port in the front of the magazine. In other guns, an outer magazine tube encircles a separate inner tube, which is removed, filled with cartridges, and then reinstalled in the gun to accomplish loading. Whatever the design, tubular-magazine semi-automatic rifles should be loaded in accord with the manufacturer's instructions.

Military-style rifles using stripper or *en bloc* clips also have model-specific loading procedures, which can be obtained from the manufacturer, firearm reference works, or a knowledgeable person such as a gunsmith or NRA Certified Instructor.

Loading a Cartridge into the Chamber

Next, with the rifle still pointed in a safe direction, held firmly in the support hand, the firing hand grasps the bolt handle or charging handle and retracts it. This may present difficulties if the gun has a strong recoil spring; it may be acceptable, under these circumstances, to brace the butt against the shoulder, as long as the rifle is maintained in a safe direction. Note that a few semi-automatic rifles have charging handles on the top or left side of of the receiver, allowing bolt retraction with the support hand.

Retracting the bolt handle or charging handle allows the top cartridge in the magazine to rise to a position where it can be fed into the chamber when the bolt goes forward. The normal procedure is to retract the bolt fully and then release it to fly forward to chamber a round. Alternatively, the bolt may be locked back using the bolt release lever. When loading is desired, the bolt release is pressed, releasing

Loading a cartridge into the chamber

Chapter 5: Semi-Automatic Rifle Parts and Operation

the bolt to fly forward. With either procedure, the forward-moving bolt will strip the top cartridge from the magazine and chamber it.

It is critical to avoid easing the bolt forward or following it down with the hand. Semi-automatic rifles are designed to function best when the bolt travels rapidly forward under the pressure of the recoil spring. Easing the bolt down is very likely to produce feeding malfunctions.

Once a live cartridge has been chambered, the shooter may commence firing. If there is to be a delay in firing, the rifle should be made safe by either engaging the safety or, if firing is to be postponed for a considerable period of time, unloading the rifle.

FIRING

Firing the loaded semi-automatic rifle involves, first, assuming the desired shooting position, and mounting the gun against the shoulder. With the trigger finger outside the trigger guard, the rifle is then taken from the "safe" condition to the "fire" condition.

The rifle is then aligned with the target. At this time, the trigger finger may enter the trigger guard and contact the trigger, and the sequence of events that culminate in firing a shot can begin.

Upon firing the first shot, the shooter may continue to fire a number of shots or may elect to lower the rifle. Alternatively, the shooter may put the loaded rifle on the shooting bench. If the gun is simply lowered, and another shot is to be immediately fired, there is no need to engage the safety. On the other hand, a loaded rifle placed on a bench should, at the very least, have its safety put into the "safe" condition. Also, if the rifle is put on the shooting bench and the shooter intends to walk away from it for any reason, even for a moment, the rifle should be fully unloaded and left on the bench with the action open and the magazine removed.

Firing a semi-automatic rifle: Align the sights with the target (A), disengage the safety (B, C). Apply increasing pressure to the trigger until the rifle fires (D).

UNLOADING

Unloading Semi-Automatic Rifles with Detachable Magazines

To unload a semi-automatic rifle with a detachable magazine, first ensure that it is pointed in a safe direction. Remove the trigger finger from the trigger and place it outside the trigger guard, alongside the receiver or stock. Next, press the magazine release button to drop the magazine from the gun. This may be located in a variety of positions, most often just forward of the trigger guard, or, on military-style semi-automatics, on the side of the receiver. As with other rifle controls, some firearms offer ambidextrous magazine releases that are equally convenient for both right- and left-hand users.

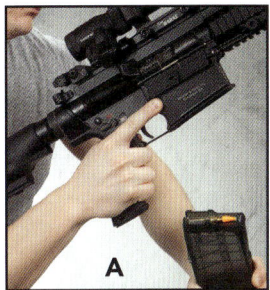 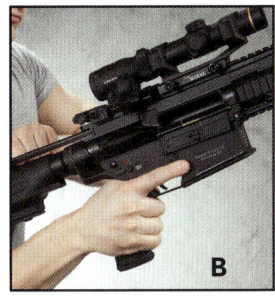 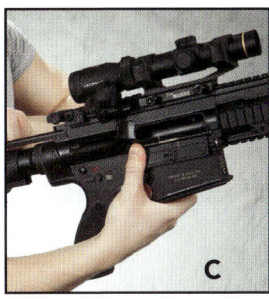

Unloading a semi-automatic rifle with a detachable magazine: Remove magazine (A), cycle the action (B), visually inspect the rifle is unloaded (C).

Once the magazine is removed from the rifle, it is still necessary to extract the live cartridge from the chamber. With the rifle still pointed in a safe direction, and the trigger finger remaining outside the trigger guard, use the firing hand to sharply retract the bolt handle or charging handle fully to the rear. This will extract the live round from the chamber and eject it. At this time, lock the bolt to the rear and visually and physically inspect the chamber to ensure the rifle is unloaded.

Unloading Semi-Automatic Rifles with Non-Detachable Magazines

The unloading procedures to be followed with semi-automatic rifles having non-detachable magazines will vary depending upon the gun design. In some tubular-magazine models, for example, unloading is accomplished simply by removing the inner magazine tube and then retracting the bolt handle to eject any cartridge that may be in the chamber. Other magazine designs will require specific unloading procedures, which can be obtained from the manufacturer, firearm reference works, or a person such as an NRA Certified Instructor or a gunsmith.

In general, unloading any gun of this type can be accomplished simply by manually cycling the bolt until all cartridges are ejected from the gun. To do this, first ensure that the rifle is pointing in a safe direction, and that your trigger finger is outside the trigger guard, alongside the receiver. Engage the safety. With a semi-automatic rifle having the bolt handle or charging handle on the right side of the rifle, or atop the receiver, grasp the rifle's fore-end with the left hand, and, while maintaining the gun in a safe direction, use the right hand to work the bolt or charging handle rearward and forward. (Reverse this hand position if you are unloading a semi-automatic rifle with the bolt handle on the left side of the gun.) A live cartridge will be ejected from the gun each time the bolt is cycled. When no more cartridges are ejected, unloading should be complete. Lock the bolt rearward and visually and physically verify that no cartridges remain in the internal magazine or chamber.

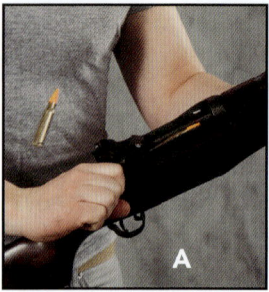 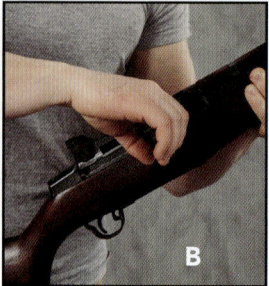 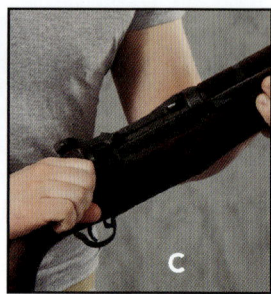

Unloading a semi-automatic rifle with a non-detachable magazine by manually cycling cartridges through the action: Pull action to the rear (A), repeat until magazine is empty (B), visually and physically inspect to ensure it is unloaded (C).

CHAPTER 6
Lever-Action Rifle Parts and Operation

Lever-action rifles operate by means of a finger-lever that is rotated downward and returned upward to perform the cycle of operation. The lever-action design has been around for more than 140 years, and conjures up images of the Old West. The lever action offered a much greater rate of fire than the single-shot rifles of the time.

Lever-action rifles consist of a *receiver*, a *bolt* which can freely move in the fore-and-aft direction, a *barrel* attached to the forward end of the receiver, a rotating *finger lever*

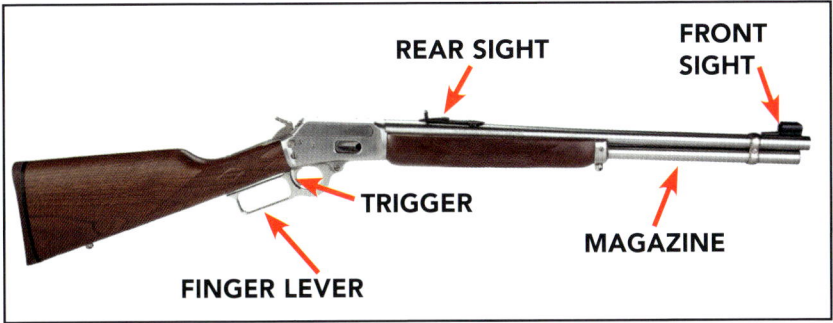

Typical lever-action rifle, right side, with major parts indicated.

below the receiver that is connected to the bolt by means of a linkage, a detachable box or integral tubular *magazine*, a *stock*, and a *trigger mechanism*. On rifles with tubular magazines, a *carrier* lifts cartridges from the magazine to a position in line with the chamber, so that the forward-moving bolt can feed them into the chamber.

Bolt lockup is accomplished in several different ways. In some designs chambered for black-powder revolver cartridges or rimfire ammunition, the linkage attached to the finger lever serves to close and lock the action. In other models, one or two vertically-sliding locking bolts locks the bolt to the receiver when the action is closed, and are lowered out of engagement when the finger lever is pulled downward. Alternately, some designs feature a breechblock that tilts upward to lock against a shoulder or recess in the receiver. Finally, in some modern designs, multi-lug rotary bolts lock into a barrel extension, giving sufficient strength to handle the most powerful contemporary cartridges.

The bolt also houses the *firing pin* and claw *extractor*. Ejection is often by means of a spring-loaded plunger in the bolt face, or, alternatively, by a fixed blade or finger mounted in the receiver. In most designs, the receiver is open on top or the side to facilitate case ejection. This opening in the receiver allows empty cartridge cases to exit the action, or to load a fresh cartridge directly into the chamber. In most lever-action designs, ignition is by way of an external hammer.

Lever-action rifles utilizing detachable magazines also feature a *magazine catch* or *magazine release*. This is a button or latch that, when depressed, releases the magazine from the gun.

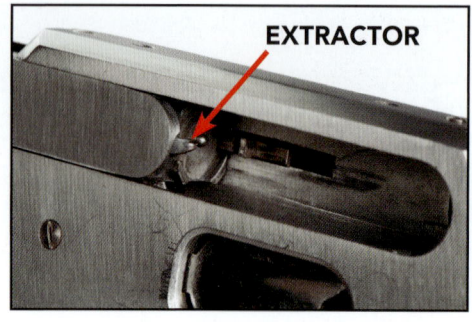

Right side of lever-action, showing bolt face

LEVER-ACTION OPERATING PRINCIPLES

The salient feature of the lever-action rifle is its rounded finger lever, integral with the trigger guard. The finger lever, hinged at the front, is connected via a linkage to either the bolt directly or to the bolt carrier (in guns of that design). In guns with tubular magazines, the finger lever linkage is also connected to the carrier so that a cartridge released from the magazine on the finger lever down-stroke will be lifted by the carrier to be aligned with the chamber on the up-stroke, facilitating feeding.

The finger lever linkage is also connected to the rifle's locking mechanism, whether it involves a locking link, locking blocks, or, as in the modern designs, a bolt carrier that contains a multi-lug rotary bolt head. With this system, lowering the finger lever moves the bolt carrier to the rear, which in turn causes, through cams, the bolt head to rotate and unlock from the barrel extension. As the finger lever is fully lowered and the bolt and carrier move further to the rear, the empty case is extracted and ejected, and the hammer is cocked.

The mechanism of feeding is determined by the type of magazine found in the gun. With tubular magazines, as the finger lever is lowered, a fresh cartridge is released from the magazine and slides atop the carrier. An internal mechanism, usually involving a component called a *cartridge stop*, ensures that only one cartridge is released from the magazine tube each time the lever is cycled. Further lowering of the finger lever lifts the shell from the magazine to a position in-line with the chamber. Pulling the finger lever upward causes the bolt to move forward and push the cartridge into the chamber, and the action to be closed and locked.

With rifles feeding from detachable box magazines, the forward movement of the carrier and bolt as the finger lever is lifted causes the bolt to strip the top cartridge from the magazine and feed it into the chamber.

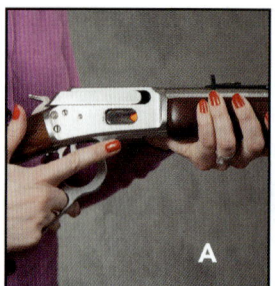 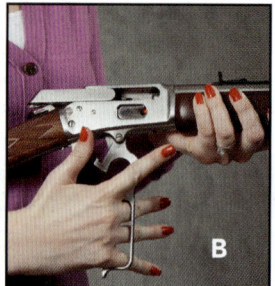 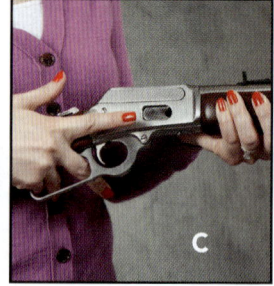

Lever-action rifle operation: Pushing lever to disengage action (A), action open, bolt cocking hammer (B), pulling lever and closing action (C).

LEVER-ACTION RIFLE MAGAZINES

Many lever-action rifles have *tubular magazines,* which are most commonly located beneath the barrel. Rifles for .22 rimfire cartridges often have tubular magazines loaded by way of an opening at the forward end of the magazine tube. Tubular-magazine lever-actions chambered for centerfire revolver or rifle cartridges usually have a spring-loaded gate in the right side of the receiver that allows cartridges to be fed into the magazine from the breech end of the tube.

Some lever-action rifles utilize detachable *box magazines,* which afford more rapid reloading than other types of magazines. Box magazines typically have a steel, aluminum or plastic *body* which houses the cartridges and the magazine's internal components. At the bottom of the magazine is a *floorplate,* usually of the same material. This is often removable to allow magazine cleaning. Inside the magazine are the *magazine spring* and *follower,* which together push the cartridges in the magazine upward into position for reliable feeding.

LEVER-ACTION TRIGGER MECHANISMS

Lever-action rifles achieve ignition most often by way of an external hammer, although internal hammers are found on a few designs. In most modern rifles of this type, the hammer is retained by a *sear,* which in turn is released by the trigger. In older designs, the external hammer is retained in the cocked position by the direct action of the trigger piece. As with other rifles, triggers for lever-action rifles may be of single-stage or two-stage design.

LEVER-ACTION SAFETY MECHANISMS

Many lever-action rifles, particularly those based on older, 19th-century designs, lack any safety lever or other sort of active safety. With these guns, all of exposed-hammer design, simply lowering the hammer was thought to be an adequate way to put them into a safe condition.

Lever-action rifles with internal hammers have safety controls, such as a sliding safety piece on the tang (rear extension) of the receiver, or a crossbolt to the front or rear of the trigger guard.

Passive safety systems include mechanisms to keep the firing pin from striking the primer unless the bolt is fully closed,

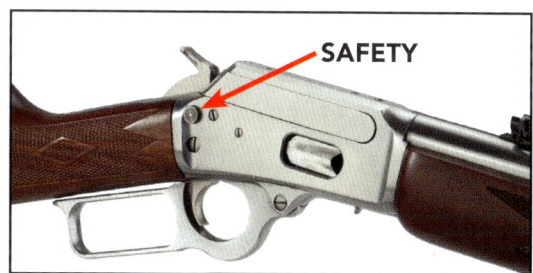

An example of a safety on a lever action rifle

as well as loaded chamber indicators. Also seen on some lever guns, such as the famed Winchester Model 94, is a safety lock that prevents full rearward motion of the trigger unless the finger lever is held snugly against the bottom of the receiver. Additionally, some lever-action rifles feature an external rotating latch that can temporarily lock the finger lever closed, preventing the action from being worked.

Chapter 6: Lever-Action Rifle Parts and Operation

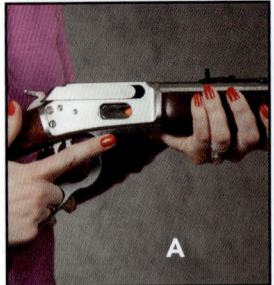
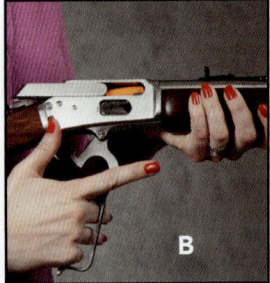
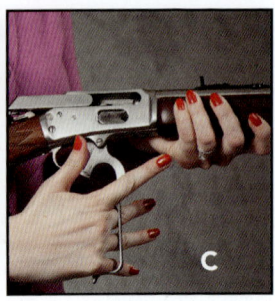
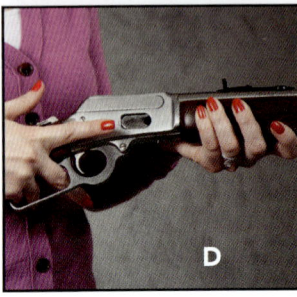

Lever-action rifle cycle of operation: Unlocking (A), extraction (B), ejection and cocking (C), feeding and locking (D).

LEVER-ACTION RIFLE CYCLE OF OPERATION

All lever-action rifles have essentially the same cycle of operation. However, some steps in the cycle may not apply to all rifles of this action type.

Firing- Pulling the trigger releases an external or internal hammer which strikes the firing pin which, in turn, hits the primer, causing the cartridge to be fired.

Unlocking— Unlocking is performed by the initial downward rotation of the finger lever, which causes the bolt to be cammed out of its locking recesses in the receiver or barrel extension.

Extraction— A claw extractor mounted on the bolt engages the rim of the cartridge case and pulls it from the chamber after the action unlocks.

Ejection— As the finger lever is lowered and the bolt moves to the rear carrying a spent cartridge case, an ejector—usually a plunger in the bolt face or a standing blade or finger mounted in the receiver—pushes on the case head, throwing the case out of the action.

Cocking— As the finger lever is further lowered, the bolt (or bolt carrier) moves sufficiently rearward to cock the hammer, which is held rearward against spring tension by the trigger mechanism.

Feeding— With tubular-magazine rifles, lowering the finger lever releases a fresh cartridge from the magazine onto the carrier, which lifts it into alignment with the chamber. As the finger lever rises and the bolt returns forward, the bolt pushes the cartridge on the carrier into the chamber. With guns fed from detachable magazines, as the finger lever rises the bolt strips a cartridge from the magazine and feeds it into the chamber.

Locking— Locking occurs as the lever is fully raised and the rifle's locking mechanism—vertically sliding locking bolts, rotating multi-lug bolt head or tilting breechblock—engages the locking recesses in the receiver, bolt or barrel extension.

OPERATING LEVER-ACTION RIFLES

Operating lever-action rifles consists of the procedures to safely and efficiently load, fire, and unload these guns.

LOADING LEVER-ACTION RIFLES

Loading a Lever-Action Rifle with a Tubular Magazine

Tubular-magazine rifles chambered for revolver or rifle cartridges, have a spring powered *loading gate* in the right side of the receiver. With the gun held in the left hand, a cartridge is held in the fingers of the right hand, and is brought to the gate with the bullet facing forward. The bullet tip is used to press the gate inward until the cartridge can be pushed fully into the magazine. When the head of the cartridge is pushed past the gate, it is secured in the magazine and the gate closes. This process is repeated until the magazine is full.

Avoid loading tubular magazines with centerfire cartridges having pointed bullets. Recoil can violently jostle the cartridges in the magazine, potentially causing a pointed bullet tip to strike and set off the primer of the cartridge ahead of it. In general, tubular magazines should only be loaded with cartridges having round- or flat-nose bullets, or bullets having soft polymer tips specifically designed for use in tubular magazines.

Cartridges are pressed into the loading gate and repeated until the magazine is full.

Lever-action .22 rimfire rifles with tubular magazines may have a receiver-mounted loading gate for loading cartridges, or may have an opening at the end of the magazine through which cartridges may be loaded. Additionally, the tubular magazines of such guns may be located in the familiar position under the barrel. These guns should be loaded in accord with the specific instructions in the owner's manual. If no owner's manual is available, one may be obtainable from the manufacturer, or a competent gunsmith may be able to give you instructions on the proper loading procedure.

LOADING THE LEVER-ACTION RIFLE MAGAZINE

The magazine should be grasped by the fingers of the support (non-firing) hand, with the top of the magazine facing upward and the front of the magazine oriented toward the firing hand. The firing hand picks up a live cartridge and brings it to the top of the

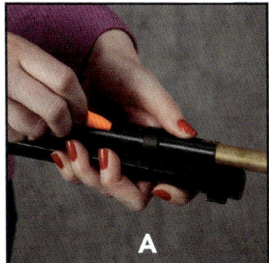
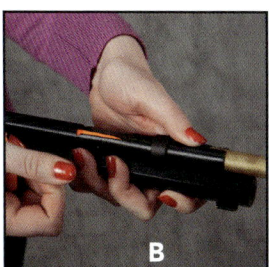
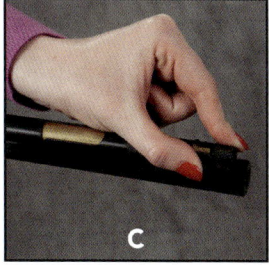

Loading a lever-action rifle with a tubular magazine: With the magazine tube open, cartridges are placed in the magazine opening (A), this is repeated until the magazine is full (B), magazine tube is closed and locked (C).

Chapter 6: Lever-Action Rifle Parts and Operation

magazine, with the case head facing the magazine and the bullet pointing away from the magazine. The case rim is used to depress the magazine follower slightly, and the cartridge is then slid under the feed lips of the magazine all the way to the rear. The case rim of the next cartridge to be loaded depresses the top cartridge in the magazine, and itself is slid under the magazine feed lips. This process is repeated for each cartridge until the magazine is loaded. Finally, the shooter should slap the rear of the loaded magazine sharply, to ensure that all cartridges are positioned to the rear for proper feeding.

Loading a Lever-Action Rifle with a Detachable Magazine

The rifle is grasped with the firing hand, with the trigger finger outside the trigger guard, alongside the frame. With the rifle pointing in a safe direction, the support hand brings the magazine to the magazine well under the receiver of the gun, and inserts the magazine fully. The magazine must be inserted in the proper orientation, with the bullets facing forward. Normally, a click is heard when the magazine is fully seated. The shooter may also slap the floorplate or basepad to ensure proper seating.

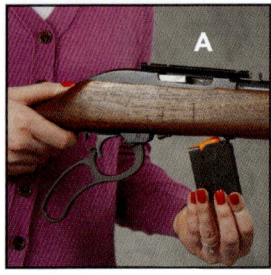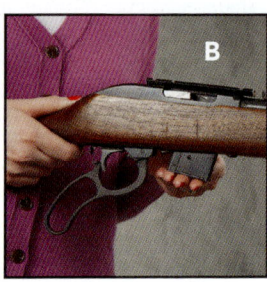

Loading a lever-action rifle with a detachable magazine: With the cartridges facing forward the magazine is placed into the magazine well (A). The magazine is pushed upward until the magazine catch is engaged (B).

Loading a Cartridge into the Chamber

Next, with the rifle still pointed in a safe direction, held firmly in the support hand, grasp the finger lever with the firing hand and pull it all the way downward, and then return it upward firmly to chamber a fresh cartridge.

Once a cartridge has been chambered, the shooter may commence firing. If there is to be a delay in firing, the rifle should be made safe by either engaging the safety or, if firing is to be postponed for a considerable period of time, unloading the rifle.

FIRING

Firing the loaded lever-action rifle involves, first, assuming the desired shooting position, and mounting the gun against the shoulder. With the trigger finger outside the trigger guard, the rifle is then taken from the "safe" condition to the "fire" condition (if a safety is available).

The rifle is then aligned with the target. At this time, the trigger finger may enter the trigger guard and contact the trigger, and the sequence of events that culminate in firing a shot can begin.

DECOCKING

When shooting a lever-action rifle having an external hammer, it may sometimes be desired to lower the cocked hammer, as during a lull in shooting.

To decock a lever-action rifle, first ensure that the rifle is pointed in a safe direction, and the trigger finger is outside of the trigger guard. Next, place the support-hand thumb between the cocked hammer and the receiver. Control the hammer spur with the thumb of the firing hand, and pull the trigger, carefully lowering the hammer until it contacts the support-hand thumb. Remove the trigger finger from the trigger and place it outside the trigger guard, alongside the frame. While still controlling the hammer spur with the firing-hand thumb, remove the support-hand thumb from between the hammer and receiver, and lower the hammer slowly the rest of the way down.

With some lever-action designs, the hammer, when fully lowered, rests against the firing pin, creating the potential for an unintended discharge of the rifle if the hammer is violently struck. In such guns, lowering the hammer to the half-cock position, if available, may confer an additional margin of safety.

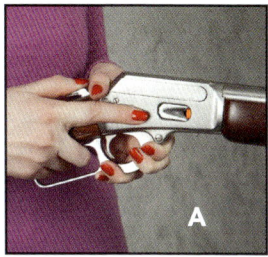 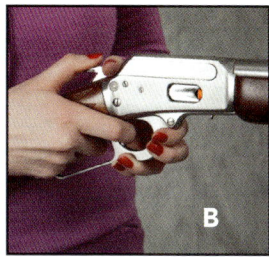 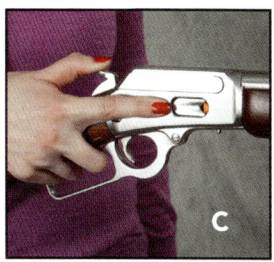

Steps in decocking a lever-action rifle: Place support hand thumb between hammer and receiver (A), control hammer spur with other thumb and pull trigger (B). Remove finger from trigger and continue to lower hammer (C).

UNLOADING

Most lever-action rifles feed from tubular magazines, with a few utilizing detachable magazines. There are specific procedures for unloading both types of rifles.

Unloading Lever-Action Rifles With Tubular Magazines

To unload lever-action rifles having tubular magazines, first ensure that the rifle is pointed in a safe direction, and that the trigger finger is outside the trigger guard. Engage the safety of the rifle (if the lever can be worked with the safety engaged). Grasp the rifle fore-end with the support hand and the finger lever with the firing hand, and work each cartridge in the magazine through the action by repeatedly lowering and raising the lever. During this process, the rifle must be kept pointing in a safe direction at all times.

After all cartridges in the magazine have been worked through the action, visually and physically inspect the magazine and chamber to ensure that the rifle is completely unloaded.

Specific rifles may have additional or alternative procedures for unloading; these will be found in the rifle's owner's manual.

Unloading Lever-Action Rifles With Detachable Magazines

To unload a lever-action rifle with a detachable magazine, first ensure that it is pointed in a safe direction. Remove the trigger finger from the trigger and place it outside the trigger guard, alongside the receiver. Next, press the magazine release button to drop the magazine from the gun. This may be located in a variety of positions—most often just forward of the trigger guard.

Chapter 6: Lever-Action Rifle Parts and Operation

Once the magazine is removed from the rifle, it is still necessary to extract the live cartridge from the chamber. With the rifle kept pointed in a safe direction, and the trigger finger still outside the trigger guard, use the firing hand to pull the finger lever all the way down. This will extract the live cartridge from the chamber and eject it. At this time, with the bolt fully rearward, visually and physically inspect the chamber to ensure the rifle is unloaded.

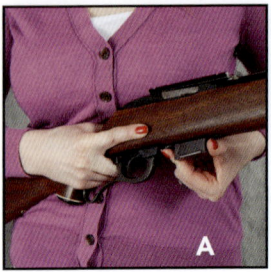 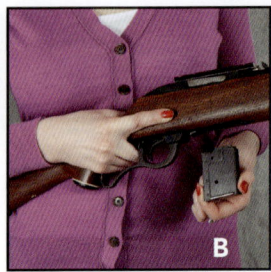 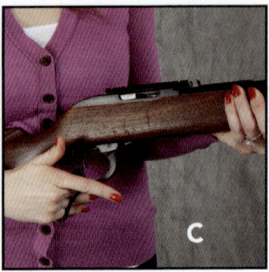

Unloading a lever-action rifle with a box magazine. Release magazine (A), remove the magazine (B), cycle the action to remove cartridge from the chamber (C).

CHAPTER 7
Slide-Action Rifle Parts and Operation

Slide-action (sometimes also called *pump-action*) rifles operate in a manner virtually identical to pump-action shotguns, in that a moveable fore-end is pulled back and returned forward to perform the cycle of operation.

Slide-action rifles fundamentally consist of a *receiver*, a *bolt* which can freely move in the fore-and-aft direction, a *barrel* attached to the forward end of the receiver, a sliding *fore-end* which is connected to an *action bar* or *bars* that enter the receiver and serve to work the action, a detachable or tubular *magazine*, a *stock*, and a *trigger mechanism*. On rifles with tubular magazines, a *carrier* lifts cartridges from the magazine to a position in line with the chamber, so that the forward-moving bolt can feed them into the chamber.

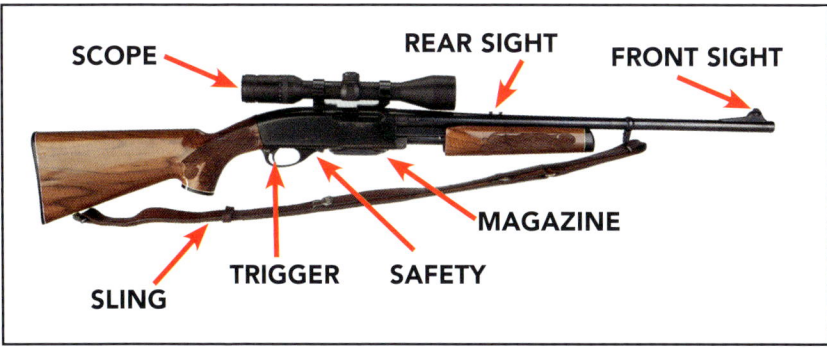

Typical slide-action rifle, left side, with major parts indicated.

The bolt also houses the *firing pin* and claw *extractor*. Ejection is often by means of a spring-loaded plunger in the bolt face, or, alternatively, by a fixed blade or finger mounted in the receiver. An *ejection port* in the receiver allows empty cartridges to exit the action, or to load a fresh cartridge directly into the chamber. Ignition is by either an internal or external hammer.

Slide-action rifles utilizing detachable magazines also feature a *magazine catch* or *magazine release*, This is a button or latch that, when depressed, releases the magazine from the gun.

SLIDE-ACTION OPERATING PRINCIPLES

Slide-action rifles feature an *action slide* or *fore-end tube* which fits inside the fore-end, and around another tube beneath the barrel. This tube can be the tubular magazine, or, in guns feeding from detachable box magazines, a separate *action tube* is used. This has the sole function of stabilizing and guiding the movement of the sliding fore-end.

Projecting back from the action slide are one or two action bars, which extend rearward into the receiver through tunnels in its front face. In some models the action bar or

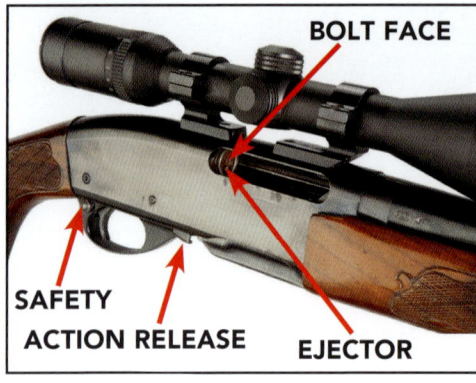

Right side of slide-action rifle, showing major parts

bars act on the bolt directly to cam it out of engagement with locking recesses in the receiver. This pattern is often found on slide-action rifles chambered for .22 rimfire cartridges. In guns chambered for more powerful centerfire cartridges, the action bars typically act upon a *bolt carrier,* which contains a multi-lug bolt that locks into the barrel extension. Rearward movement of the fore-end and action bars impels the carrier to the rear, which in turn causes, through cams, the bolt head to rotate and unlock from the barrel extension. As the slide is pulled further to the rear, the bolt extracts and ejects the empty case, and cocks the hammer.

The mechanism of feeding is determined by the type of magazine found in the gun. With tubular magazines, as the slide is retracted, an internal mechanism releases a fresh cartridge from the magazine. A *cartridge stop* ensures that only one cartridge is released each time the action is cycled. The released cartridge slides atop the *carrier,* which lifts the shell from the magazine to a position in-line with the chamber. Pulling the slide forward causes the bolt to push the shell into the chamber and close and lock the action.

With rifles feeding from detachable box magazines, forward movement of the fore-end pulls the bolt forward, allowing it to strip the top cartridge from the magazine and feed it into the chamber.

Many slide-action rifles have an *action bar lock,* an internal mechanism that prevents the slide from being moved rearward to unlock the action unless the trigger has been pulled. This ensures that a shooter, after chambering a round, is prevented from unlocking the action by inadvertently pulling on the fore-end. An action bar lock lever, sometimes on the left lower side of the receiver, is pressed to release the action bars.

SLIDE-ACTION RIFLE MAGAZINES

Many slide-action rifles utilize detachable *box magazines,* which afford one of the main advantages of such arms: rapid reloading. Box magazines typically have a steel, aluminum or plastic *body* which houses the cartridges and the magazine's internal components. At the bottom of the magazine is a *floorplate,* usually of the same material. This is often removable to allow magazine cleaning. Inside the magazine are the *magazine spring* and *follower,* which together push the cartridges in the magazine upward into position for reliable feeding.

Some .22 rimfire slide-action rifles will be encountered with *tubular magazines.* These are almost always located beneath the barrel. These magazines are loaded by way of an opening in the forward end of the tube.

SLIDE-ACTION TRIGGER MECHANISMS

Slide-action rifles achieve ignition by way of either an internal or external hammer. In most modern designs, the hammer is retained by a *sear*, which in turn is released by the trigger. In older designs, the external hammer is retained in the cocked position by the direct action of the trigger piece. As with other rifles, triggers for slide-action rifles may be of single-stage or two-stage design.

SLIDE-ACTION SAFETY MECHANISMS

The *active*, or user-operated, safety systems of slide-action rifles most commonly take the form of a crossbolt safety located at the front or rear of the trigger guard. When moved to "safe," the crossbolt blocks the trigger.

Passive safety systems include mechanisms to keep the firing pin from striking the primer unless the bolt is fully closed, and to prevent the hammer from falling as the slide is worked even if the trigger is still depressed. If the action cycles while the trigger is still held rearward, it must be released by the trigger finger and then pulled again to fire the next shot.

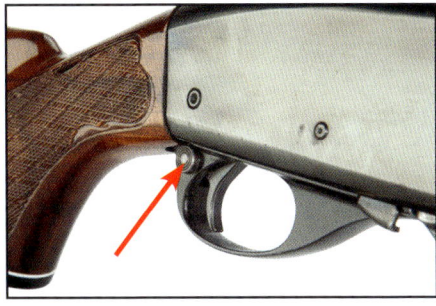

Typical slide-action rifle safety control

SLIDE-ACTION RIFLE CYCLE OF OPERATION

All slide-action rifles have essentially the same cycle of operation. However, some steps in the cycle may not apply to all action types.

Firing— Pulling the trigger releases an internal or external hammer which strikes the firing pin which, in turn hits the primer, causing the cartridge to be fired.

Unlocking— Unlocking is performed by the initial retraction of the slide, which causes the bolt to be cammed out of its locking recesses in the receiver or barrel extension.

Extraction— A claw extractor mounted on the bolt engages the rim of the cartridge case and pulls it from the chamber after the action unlocks.

Ejection— As the fore-end and bolt move to the rear carrying a spent cartridge case, an ejector—usually a plunger in the bolt face or a standing blade or finger mounted in the receiver—pushes on the case head, throwing the case out of the action through the ejection port.

Cocking— At or near the extreme rearward limit of slide travel, the bolt (or bolt carrier) cocks the hammer, which is held rearward against spring tension by the trigger mechanism.

Feeding— With tubular-magazine rifles, retracting the fore-end releases a fresh cartridge from the magazine onto the carrier, which lifts it into alignment with the chamber. As the fore-end and bolt return forward, the bolt pushes the cartridge on the carrier into the

Chapter 7: Slide-Action Rifle Parts and Operation

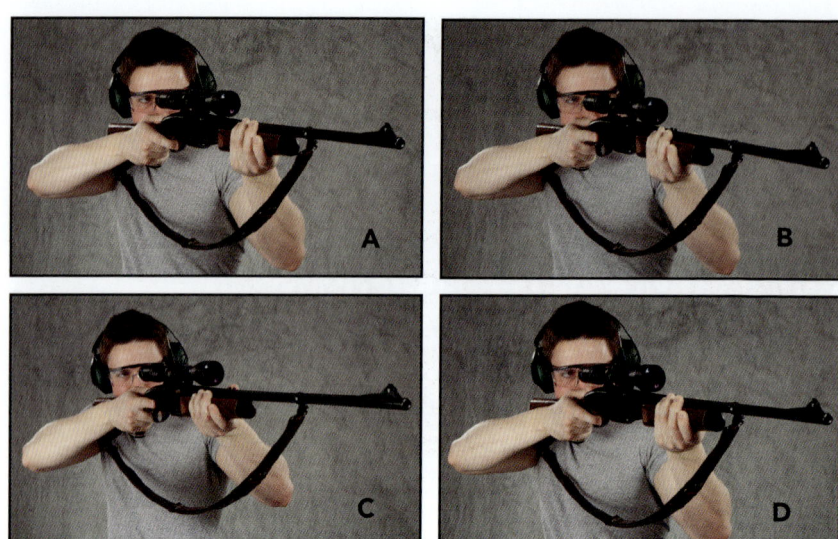

Slide-action rifle cycle of operation: Firing (A), unlocking (B), extraction and ejection (C), feeding and locking (D).

chamber. With guns fed from detachable magazines, as the fore-end is returned forward, the bolt strips a cartridge from the magazine and feeds it into the chamber.

Locking— Locking occurs as the fore-end and bolt return fully forward, and the bolt is cammed so that its lugs or body engage their locking recesses in the barrel extension of the receiver.

OPERATING SLIDE-ACTION RIFLES

Operating slide-action rifles consists of the procedures to safely and efficiently load, fire, and unload these guns.

LOADING

Loading means filling an empty gun with cartridges. With guns having detachable magazines, this first requires that the magazine be loaded.

LOADING DETACHABLE SLIDE-ACTION RIFLE MAGAZINES

The magazine should be grasped by the fingers of the support (non-firing) hand, with the top of the magazine facing upward and the front of the magazine oriented toward the firing hand. The firing hand picks up a live cartridge and brings it to the top of the magazine, with the case head facing the magazine and the bullet pointing away from the magazine. The case rim is used to depress the magazine follower slightly, and the cartridge is then slid under the feed lips of the magazine all the way to the rear. The case rim of the next cartridge to be loaded depresses the top cartridge in the magazine, and itself is slid

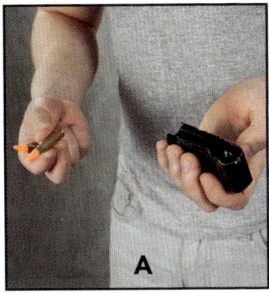 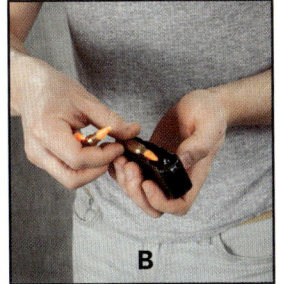 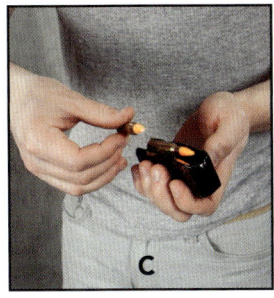

Loading slide-action rifle magazines: Start with an empty magazine with a live cartridge in hand (A), continue adding live cartridges to the magazine (B), repeat until the magazine is full (C).

under the magazine feed lips. This process is repeated for each cartridge until the magazine is loaded. Finally, the shooter should slap the rear of the loaded magazine sharply, to ensure that all cartridges are positioned to the rear of the unit, for proper feeding.

LOADING SLIDE-ACTION RIFLES

Loading a Rifle with a Detachable Magazine

The rifle is grasped with the firing hand, with the trigger finger outside the trigger guard, alongside the frame. With the rifle pointing in a safe direction, the support hand brings the magazine to the magazine well under the receiver of the gun, and inserts the magazine fully. The magazine must be inserted in the proper orientation, with the bullets facing forward. Normally, a click is heard when the magazine is fully seated. The shooter may also slap the floorplate or basepad to ensure proper seating.

Loading a Rifle with a Non-Detachable Magazine

Rifles having non-detachable magazines, such as tubular-magazine .22 rimfire rifles, may be loaded in a number of ways. Some can be loaded by way of a loading port at the end of the magazine, while others have an inner magazine tube which is removed, filled with cartridges, and then reinserted into the outer magazine tube in the rifle. Such rifles should be loaded in accord with the specific instructions in the owner's manual. If no owner's manual is available, one may be obtainable from the manufacturer, or a competent gunsmith may be able to give you instructions on the proper loading procedure.

Loading a Cartridge into the Chamber

Next, with the rifle still pointed in a safe direction, held firmly in the firing hand with the trigger finger outside the trigger guard, alongside the receiver, grasp the fore-end with the support hand and pull it all the way to the rear, and then return it firmly forward to chamber a fresh cartridge.

Work the slide-action smartly, to avoid jams or incomplete bolt lockup. On rifles having an action bar lock, it may be necessary to deactivate the lock to retract the fore-end, if the trigger was previously pulled.

Once a live cartridge has been chambered, the shooter may commence firing. If there is to be a delay in firing, the rifle should be made safe by either engaging the safety or, if firing is to be postponed for a considerable period of time, unloading the rifle.

Chapter 7: Slide-Action Rifle Parts and Operation

FIRING

Firing the loaded slide-action rifle involves, first, assuming the desired shooting position, and mounting the gun against the shoulder. With the trigger finger outside the trigger guard, the rifle is then taken from the "safe" condition to the "fire" condition.

The rifle is then aligned with the target. At this time, the trigger finger may enter the trigger guard and contact the trigger, and the sequence of events that culminate in firing a shot can begin.

Upon firing a shot, the shooter may continue to fire, may elect to lower the rifle or put the loaded rifle on the shooting bench. If the gun is simply lowered, and another shot is to be immediately fired, there is no need to engage the safety. On the other hand, a loaded rifle placed on a bench should at least be put into the "safe" condition, and should be completely unloaded if the shooter intends to leave it for any length of time.

DECOCKING

When shooting a slide-action rifle having an external hammer, it may be desired to lower the hammer, as during a lull in shooting.

To decock a slide-action rifle, first ensure that the rifle is pointed in a save direction, and the trigger finger is outside of the trigger guard. Next, place the support-hand thumb between the cocked hammer and the receiver. Control the hammer spur with the thumb of the firing hand, and pull the trigger, carefully lowering it to contact the support-hand thumb. Remove the trigger finger from the trigger and place it outside the trigger guard, alongside the frame. While still controlling the hammer spur with the firing-hand thumb, remove the support-hand thumb from between the hammer and receiver, and lower the hammer slowly the rest of the way down.

In some cases, the fully lowered hammer rests directly on the firing pin, creating the potential for an inadvertent discharge if the hammer is forcefully struck. This hazard may be decreased by lowering the hammer only to the half-cock position (on guns that offer this feature).

UNLOADING

Almost all slide-action rifles have either tubular or detachable box magazines. There are different unloading procedures for each magazine type.

Unloading Slide-Action Rifles with Tubular Magazines

Most slide-action rifles with tubular magazines are chambered for .22 rimfire cartridges, with the magazine located under the barrel. Such rifles can be unloaded by simply working all the cartridges in the magazine through the action.

First ensure that the rifle is pointed in a safe direction, and remove your trigger finger from the trigger and place it outside the trigger guard, alongside the receiver. Grasp the fore-end and work it back and forth as needed to cycle all the cartridges through the action. With some guns, it may first be necessary to engage an action release lever before the fore-end can be retracted. While cycling live cartridges through the action, keep the rifle pointed in a safe direction and your trigger finger outside the trigger guard. When no cartridges are ejected from the action when the fore-end is cycled, the rifle is unload-

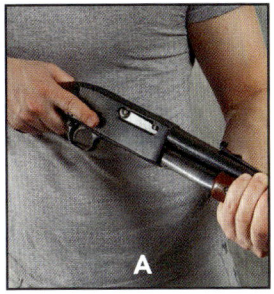 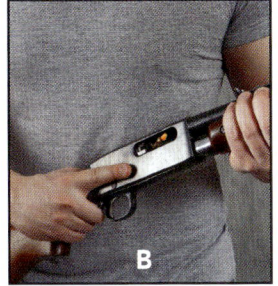 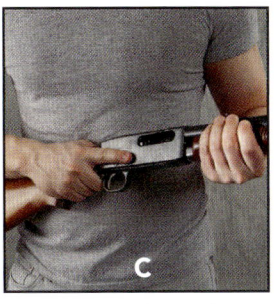

Unloading a slide-action rifle with a tubular magazine: Slide action to the rear (A), eject live cartridge from chamber (B), continue to cycle the action until rifle is unloaded (C).

ed. Retract the fore-end and visually and physically verify that the chamber is empty and that no cartridges remain in the magazine.

Some slide-action .22 rimfire rifles have magazine tubes which may be unloaded from the front. With such guns, follow the instructions in the owner's manual, or consult a knowledgeable person, such as a gunsmith or NRA Certified Instructor, for the proper unloading procedure.

Unloading Slide-Action Rifles with Detachable Magazines

To unload a slide-action rifle with a detachable magazine, first ensure that it is pointed in a safe direction. Remove the trigger finger from the trigger and place it outside the trigger guard, alongside the frame. Next, press the magazine release button to drop the magazine from the gun. This may be located in a variety of positions—most often just forward of the trigger guard.

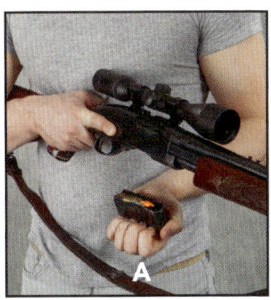 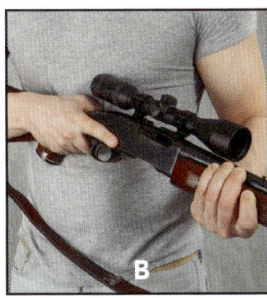

Unloading a slide-action rifle with a detachable magazine: Remove magazine (A), cycle action to remove cartridge from chamber (B).

Once the magazine is removed from the rifle, it is still necessary to extract the live cartridge from the chamber. With the rifle kept pointed in a safe direction, and the trigger finger still outside the trigger guard, use the firing hand to retract the fore-end fully to the rear. This will extract the live round from the chamber and eject it. At this time, with the bolt fully rearward, visually and physically inspect the chamber to ensure the rifle is unloaded.

CHAPTER 8
Other Types of Rifle Actions

In addition to the four major types of rifle actions discussed in the preceding chapters—bolt-action, semi-automatic, lever-action and pump-action—there are also several other types of actions that may be encountered. Two of the most common of these are the *falling block* and *break-action*.

FALLING-BLOCK ACTION

The falling-block action dates back to the 19th century, and is a single-shot in which a rising and falling breechblock is used to close and lock the action. While the design is more than 150 years old, it is still popular among varmint shooters and big-game hunters. Falling-block actions can be extremely strong, able to handle modern high-intensity cartridges, and the rigid barrel-to-receiver mounting contributes to accuracy. Additionally, the short receiver of these actions makes possible a relatively short and handy gun size.

Falling-block actions consist of a blocklike *receiver*, a *barrel* attached to the receiver, a *breechblock* that slides vertically in the receiver, a *finger lever* or *cocking lever, trigger* and *safety mechanisms,* and a two piece *stock* consisting of a *fore-end* and separate *buttstock.* Ignition is by an *internal firing pin* or *external hammer.*

To operate a falling-block action, the cocking lever is pulled downward, causing the breechblock to fall, exposing the chamber and cocking the hammer or firing pin. A fresh cartridge is inserted into the chamber and the cocking lever is pulled upward to close and lock the action. To prevent inadvertent action opening, the cocking lever is secured by a latch that must be manually disengaged before the lever can be rotated downward.

After loading, the rifle may be fired. Unloading the falling-block is accomplished by unlatching the cocking lever and rotating it downward, which causes the rifle's extractor to pull the spent shell slightly rearward out of the chamber. This shell is manually removed from the action, and, if further shooting is desired, a new cartridge is inserted into the chamber.

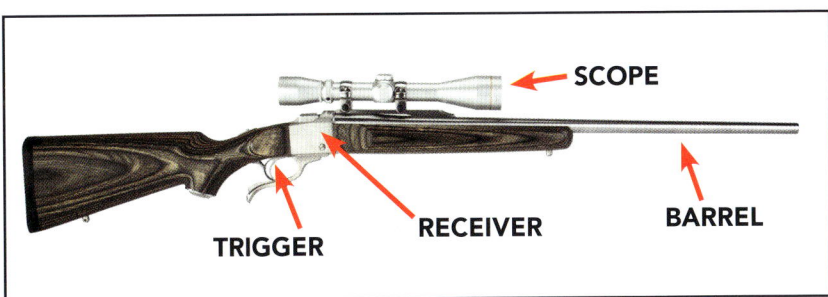

A typical falling-block rifle

Variation on the falling-block include designs in which the breechblock, instead of moving vertically in the receiver, is instead hinged at the rear. When the cocking lever is worked, the front of the breechblock rotates downward to expose the chamber, and upward to close and lock the action. In other ways such guns operate like falling-block rifles.

BREAK-ACTION

Break-action rifles are so called because the gun is "broken" open around a hinge pin at the front of the receiver. "Hinge action" is another name for the same type of action.

At one time, double-barreled break-action rifles were the preferred tool for hunting dangerous African or Asian game. Fitted with either a single trigger that would fire both barrels with successive pulls, or two triggers, these double rifles allowed the fastest possible follow-up shot. Additionally, because each barrel had its own separate firing mechanism, double rifles were thought to be more reliable than bolt-action or other rifles having only a single mechanism.

When first introduced, double rifles were chambered mostly for large, relatively low-pressure cartridges firing heavy bullets at only moderate velocities. Such rifles would not be safe to shoot with modern cartridges having chamber pressures above 60,000 pounds per square inch (p.s.i.). Some custom gunmakers still make double rifles, however, with improved metals and designs that are much stronger and able to fire higher-pressure ammunition safely. These rifles are truly among the finest examples of the gunmaker's art, but sadly are prohibitively expensive.

While the African double rifle remains the classic break-action rifle, several manufacturers currently produce economical single-barrel (single-shot) break-action rifles in contemporary chamberings. Also, some break-action guns from Europe called *drillings* combine both shotgun and rifle barrels in one firearm.

Break-action rifle closed (top) and opened (bottom)

Break-action rifles are very much like break-action shotguns in design and operation. A *receiver* contains the *action components*, and has a *hinge pin* or *trunnions* at the front, around which a removable *barrel* or *barrels* can rotate. Action lockup is by way of any number of mechanisms, including a horizontally-sliding *bolt*, retractable locking *pins*, a *crossbolt*, and so forth. The action is opened by turning a *top lever* (or, in some models, depressing a lever on the receiver), which retracts the locking mechanism and allows the action to be opened, accomplished by rotating the barrel(s) downward. Extractors pull any unfired case a short way out of the chambers, allowing manual removal.

56   *Chapter 8: Other Types of Rifle Actions*

With break-action guns having internal hammers, opening the action also forces rearward a cocking rod that cocks the hammers. Break-action rifles with external hammers are cocked manually. In either case, after a fresh cartridge has been put in the chamber(s), the action is closed by rotating the barrel or barrels upward. The rifle may then be fired.

OTHER ACTION TYPES

On occasion, other types of actions may be encountered, such as the *rolling-block* and *trapdoor Springfield*. Information on firing such rifles of historical interest should be obtained from a competent gunsmith specializing in their repair, or from reference works on these guns. Always consult a gunsmith before attempting to fire any original rifle of this type.

CHAPTER 9
Ammunition Fundamentals

While much attention is paid to rifle design and performance, shooters sometimes forget that it is the cartridge that largely determines the performance of any firearm system. Just as a computer is no more than a device for running software, a rifle is only a tool for getting the most out of a particular cartridge.

CARTRIDGE TYPES

There are two types of metallic cartridges used in modern firearms: *rimfire cartridges* and *centerfire cartridges*. These two cartridge types differ in the location of the pressure-sensitive priming mixture that ignites the gunpowder when the firing pin strikes the case head. In a rimfire cartridge, the priming mixture is contained in a fold in the cartridge rim. In a centerfire cartridge, the priming mixture is contained in a separate component called a *primer*, located in the center of the case head. These differences are explained below.

Cutaway drawings showing rimfire (l.) and centerfire cartridge cases. Priming compound is shown in green.

CARTRIDGE COMPONENTS

There are four parts to any modern cartridge: *case, powder, primer* (or *priming compound*) and *bullet*.

Case— Modern cartridge cases are generally made of brass (occasionally of steel); some are nickel-plated. The case consists of a *body*, which terminates at one end in a *neck* and *mouth*, and, at the other, in a thick *head*. A centerfire cartridge case head contains a *primer pocket* that holds the primer, and a *flash hole* that conveys the primer spark through the *web* of the case to the *powder charge*. The head also contains a *headstamp* of the cartridge name. A rimfire case head has no primer, but instead has priming compound located in a fold in the case rim (see **Primer** section on following page).

Chapter 9: Ammunition Fundamentals

There are several types of cases, based on the shapes of the body and head. Case bodies are either of *bottleneck design*, with a neck smaller than the body and a pronounced shoulder where they meet, or *straight*, with a body about the same size as the neck.

Case heads come in five configurations. *Rimmed* cases have a protruding rim that is grasped by the rifle's extractor to remove it from the chamber. *Semi-rimmed* cases have a rim that is only slightly larger than the body diameter, and an extractor groove that allows the extractor a better grip. *Rimless cases* have a deep extractor groove that creates a rim the same diameter as the case body, while *rebated-rim* cases have a rim smaller in diameter than the body. Finally, *rimless belted* cases are simply rimless cases with a thickened belt directly above the extractor groove. These are used for *magnum* cartridges (cartridges having a larger-than-normal case capacity to develop higher velocity).

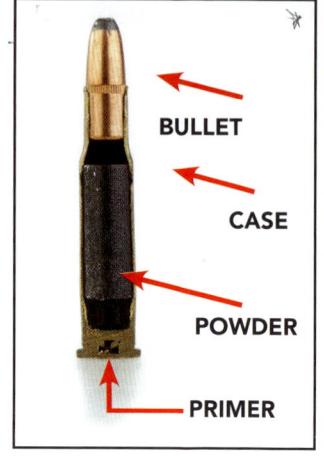

Cartridge components.

Regardless of design, all cases performs the same functions. The case contains the other cartridge components, locates the bullet in relation to the bore and rifling; and provides a combustion chamber for the burning of the propellant. Upon cartridge ignition, the case contains the pressure created by propellant gases, and, perhaps most importantly, it expands tightly against the chamber walls, preventing gas leakage to the rear. Finally, after the bullet leaves the muzzle and gas pressure drops, the case springs back slightly from the chamber walls, allowing it to be easily extracted.

Straight (l.) and bottleneck cases.

Primer— The primer creates the spark that ignites the powder charge. It is essentially a small metal *cup* containing a layer of pressure-sensitive *priming compound*, over which is placed an *anvil* whose pointed tip bears against this compound. When the trigger is pulled, the firing pin sharply hits and indents the primer cup, pushing it against the anvil. This, in turn, compresses the priming compound, igniting it and creating a spark that goes through a *flash hole* to the powder. Such primers are located in the center of the case head; cartridges so configured are thus called *center-fire* cartridges.

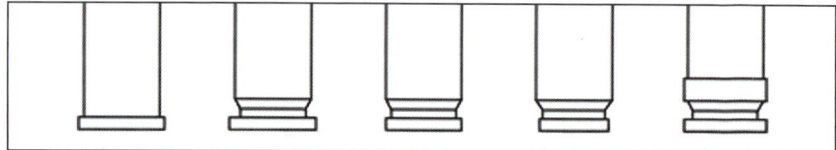

Case head types. From left, rimmed, semi-rimmed, rimless, rebated-rimless, and belted rimless.

Some cartridges lack a central primer, but instead have a thin layer of priming compound that coats the bottom of the inside of the case, including the portion of the case that is folded to create a rim. With such cartridges, the firing pin hits the exposed case rim, indenting the thin metal and compressing the priming compound to create a spark. Today's *rimfire* cartridges are limited to relatively low-power .17- and .22-cal. cartridges.

Cutaway of primer components, showing cup, priming coumpound and anvil.

Powder— Though all firearms once used black powder to propel the bullet, ammunition for modern arms use *smokeless powder*, which is made primarily of nitrocellulose (so-called *single-base powders*) or a combination of nitrocellulose and nitroglycerin (*double-base powders*). When the powder is ignited by the primer, it is rapidly converted to a large volume of hot, expanding gas that greatly increases the pressure inside the case, and pushes the bullet down the barrel at high velocity.

Smokeless powder is a propellant that burns at a controlled rate. Thus, powders for different purposes have different compositions, coatings, granule shapes and granule sizes, to produce optimal performance within safe pressure limits.

Bullet— Rifle bullets may have a variety of shapes and types of construction. Most are of lead or jacketed lead construction. In the former, the bullet is cast or swaged to the proper diameter and shape. In the latter type of construction, the bullet has a lead core surrounded by a thin copper jacket. Jacketed lead bullets can be driven to higher velocities, and can be designed to give optimum terminal performance for the intended purpose.

Gaining in popularity are solid copper bullets, particularly for hunting and defense. For hunting dangerous African game, heavy, large-caliber solid brass bullets have long been popular, as they give deep penetration.

Rifle bullet shape largely determines ballistic performance in the air, particularly at longer ranges. Sharp-pointed *spitzer* bullets have less air resistance than round-nose types, and thus have flatter *trajectories* (bullet paths) and are deflected less by crosswinds. Long range performance is also enhanced by the addition of a *boattail* to the bullet base. More information on rifle bullet performance is contained in Chapter 19: Selecting Rifles, Ammunition and Accessories.

Examples of different types of rifle bullets. Semi-jacketed round nose, full metal jacket, ballistic tip, soft point, solid lead, copper boat tail.

Chapter 9: Ammunition Fundamentals

CARTRIDGE FIRING SEQUENCE

The firing of a cartridge in a firearm follows a specific sequence of events, as shown in the accompanying drawing. Starting with a cartridge in the chamber and the breech closed (A), the trigger is pulled, causing the firing pin to hit the cartridge primer (B) or cartridge rim, in the case of rimfire cartridges. The primer explodes with a hot spark that ignites the powder in the case (C). As the powder burns, it creates high-pressure gas that begins to push the bullet down the bore (D). Increasing pressure in the chamber also causes the case to expand outward tightly against the chamber walls, preventing gas leakage to the rear. Continued combustion of the gunpowder accelerates the bullet completely through the bore (E), until it leaves the muzzle (F). The hot, high-velocity gas exiting the muzzle makes a loud "bang" when it hits the surrounding atmosphere.

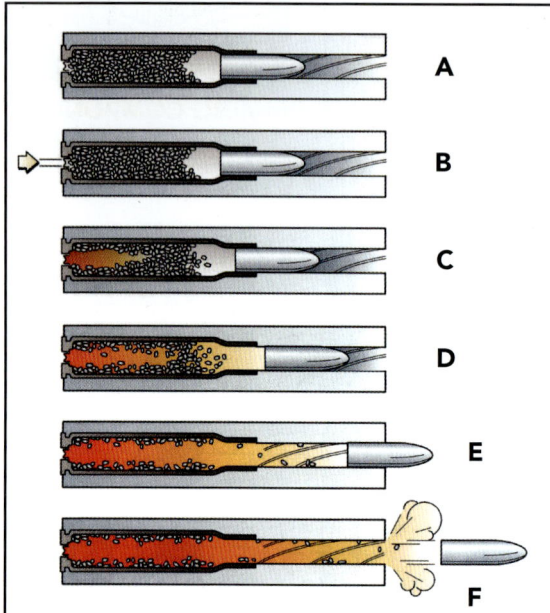

CARTRIDGE NOMENCLATURE

Cartridge nomenclature can be confusing, as there has never been a standardized procedure for naming cartridges. Basically, rifle cartridge names have two parts. The first part of the name is a number, either in millimeters or in decimal inch measurements (known as caliber), that represents either the bullet or bore diameter (often only approximately). Sometimes there are two numbers; European cartridges in particular are designated by both the bullet diameter in millimeters and the case length in millimeters (e.g., 7.62 X 51 mm).

The second part of the designation is far more variable, and may represent any of several things: the name of the company responsible for the cartridge's development (.243 Winchester); the individual (.35 Whelen) who originated or designed the cartridge; a popular or descriptive name (.220 Swift); or, with military-designed cartridges, the firearm in which it was used (.50 Browning Machine Gun). A number of cartridges have more than one name, often both decimal and metric designations, such as the .308 Winchester and 7.62 x 51 mm.

For the rifle owner to select the proper ammunition for his or her firearm, all that is required is to match the designation on the barrel or, sometimes, the receiver with that

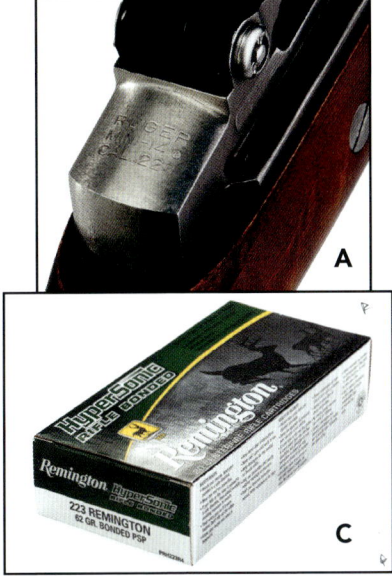
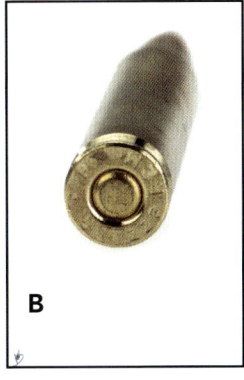

The proper ammunition for a given rifle is determined by matching the markings on the barrel or receiver (A), with the cartridge designation on the headstamp (B), and the cartridge box (C).

on the cartridge box and the cartridge headstamp. If the firearm lacks a cartridge designation, or if there is a suspicion that the rifle may have been modified to fire a cartridge other than what is indicated by the markings, the gun should be taken to a competent gunsmith for an evaluation.

AMMUNITION SAFETY

The primary factor in ammunition safety involves using the proper ammunition for the firearm. As mentioned above, you must ensure that the designation on the cartridge box, headstamp and gun barrel or receiver all match. The owner's manual may also contain information on the proper cartridges to use in your rifle.

Misfires, Hangfires and Squib Loads

There are three main ammunition problems every shooter should be aware of.

A *misfire* occurs when the cartridge fails to fire when it is struck by the firing pin. A *hangfire* occurs when a cartridge fails to fire immediately upon being hit by the firing pin, but fires after a period of time has elapsed. This can occur with contaminated ammunition, for example.

Whenever a cartridge fails to immediately ignite upon firing pin impact, the rifle should be kept pointing in a safe direction, with the action kept closed, for at least 30 seconds. After that time, the action may be opened and the faulty cartridge removed from the gun. This is done because it will not immediately be clear whether the shooter is dealing with a misfire or hangfire. Opening the action prematurely on a hangfire can result in damage to the rifle or injury to the shooter if the cartridge ignites when not confined in the chamber with the action locked.

Finally, a *squib load* occurs when the cartridge ignites, but the shooter experiences a reduced level of sound, muzzle flash or recoil. This can occur when there is insufficient powder in the case, or the powder or primer has become contaminated. Anytime a squib load is suspected, the action should be opened, the defective cartridge removed, and the bore inspected for obstructions. A squib load can result in a bullet lodged in the bore, which can produce damage to the rifle or injury to the shooter if another round is fired without clearing the obstruction.

Ammunition in Fires

Extensive tests have shown that ammunition in a fire does not explode, or propel the bullet to dangerous velocities. In general, cartridges exposed to fire will burst, propelling the bullet only a few feet. The primer may be expelled at relatively high velocity, as well as small shards of brass from the ruptured case, but these objects generally represent a danger only to the eyes, and only at very close range.

Safe Ammunition Storage

Ammunition should be stored in a cool and dry place; it can withstand the normal variations in temperature and humidity found in the typical home environment. Prolonged exposure to high temperatures is to be avoided. Also to be avoided is contamination by water, solvents, lubricants and so forth. Store ammunition in a location off the floor and protected from exposure to water, as from a leaky roof or damp basement.

Ammunition should also be stored in a manner to keep it from unauthorized persons, such as children and visitors to the home. Each gun owner has to determine what level of security is best suited for his or her environment. In some cases, the rifle owner may choose to keep ammunition in a lockable container. Most gun shops will be able to make recommendations regarding the type of container suitable for this purpose.

Disposal of Unserviceable Ammunition

Ammunition that has been in a flood or fire, has been immersed in water, or has been exposed to solvents, oils or other liquids, should not be fired. Instead, such ammunition should be considered unserviceable and must be disposed of. Never dispose of such ammunition by burying, dumping in a waterway, or selling it at a yard sale. Proper disposal methods include delivery to a hazardous materials disposal center; or return of the unserviceable ammunition to the original manufacturer.

More information on ammunition safety can be found in free brochures from the Sporting Arms and Ammunition Manufacturers' Institute (SAAMI), 11 Mile Hill Road, Newtown, CT 06470-2359.

CHAPTER 10
Clearing Rifle Stoppages

Modern rifles are generally extremely reliable; however, stoppages may occur on occasion. Each requires a separate procedure to resolve it.

Failure to feed occurs when a cartridge fails to fully enter the chamber. Sometimes the jammed cartridge can be clearly seen in the ejection port, while at other times the bolt is only a fraction of an inch short of being fully closed and locked. A failure to feed can result from problems with the ammunition, the magazine, or the gun. With guns having detachable box magazines, the procedure for clearing such stoppages involves tapping the bottom of the magazine to ensure that it is fully seated, retracting the bolt handle forcefully to eject the jammed cartridge, and then letting the bolt fly forward on a semi-automatic, or push it forward on a bolt or other action type to chamber the next round in the magazine.

Sometimes a failure to feed results when a fired cartridge case fails to be ejected from the action, and the bolt retracts enough to strip a fresh cartridge from the magazine. This can also happen by "short stroking" the slide, or lever when using a pump or lever action rifle. When this happens, the live cartridge can become jammed against the empty case in the action. Less frequently, *double feeding* may occur, in which two live cartridges become wedged together just forward of the bolt in the receiver.

Resolving either of these situations may involve removing the ammunition source, usually a magazine, and work the action several times to work the cartridge loose. If that fails, lock the bolt rearward and pry the case and/or cartridges out of the action. During this procedure the rifle must be kept pointing in a safe direction, with the trigger finger outside the trigger guard.

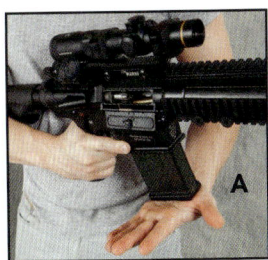  

Clearing a failure-to-feed stoppage in a semi-automatic rifle having a detachable magazine: Slap the magazine (A), cycle the action to clear jam (B), with action in battery, rifle is ready to fire (C).

A *failure to fire a chambered cartridge* can take two forms. If pulling the trigger does not cause the hammer to fall, there is most likely a problem with the gun. On the other hand, if the hammer falls on a chambered cartridge but the gun does not fire, this may be the result of defective ammunition as well as a broken or defective gun component. In either case, if you should encounter a failure to fire, keep the rifle pointed in a safe direction, with the action closed, for at least 30 seconds, to avoid the hazard of a hangfire (see

Chapter 9: Ammunition Fundamentals). After this interval you may retract the bolt sharply to extract and eject the non-firing cartridge. A lack of an indentation on the primer, or a weak indentation, may reveal a gun problem. If the primer indentation is strong, the problem is more likely with the cartridge.

A *stovepipe jam* is a type of *failure-to-eject stoppage* in which a fired case does not eject fully from the action, but ends up sticking out of the ejection port, blocking the bolt from going forward into battery. This can be produced by a faulty extractor, ejector, or underpowered recoil spring

Stovepipe jam

in a semi automatic. On occasion, a stovepipe jam may result when brass being ejected out of the ejection port strikes the overhanging windage turret of a telescopic sight, and bounces back into the port. Finally, excessive dirt in the action, or a lack of lubrication, can be enough to make ejection marginal. Stovepipe jams can be cleared by opening the action to remove the fired case, and closing it to chamber a fresh cartridge, if desired.

The last commonly encountered type of stoppage—*failure to extract and eject*—occurs when the bolt cannot be retracted, or the extractor slides past the cartridge on hinge, or falling block type rifles, and a fired case or live cartridge cannot be extracted from the chamber and ejected from the action. This may be produced by dirty, damaged or defective ammunition, or ammunition generating an unsafe level of pressure. Point the rifle in a safe direction and ensure that your trigger finger is outside the trigger guard, and give the bolt or charging handle a sharp rearward pull with the fingers, or slap with the palm of the hand. With a hinge or falling block action, you can usually remove the stuck case by pulling the case rearward with the action open. If that does not work, you may need to use a flathead screwdriver to help pry it out. If this fails to remove the case, consult a knowledgeable person, such as an NRA Certified Instructor, range officer or gunsmith.

A live cartridge and a fired case (left) can become wedged together in the receiver, preventing feeding. Less commonly, this can happen with two live cartridges (right). Clearing either stoppage involves retracting the bolt and removing the jammed cartridge(s) out of the receiver.

PART III

BUILDING RIFLE SHOOTING SKILLS

CHAPTER 11
Fundamentals of Rifle Shooting

Successful rifle shooting is based upon the fundamental principles of marksmanship. These fundamentals are *aiming, breath control, hold control, trigger control* and *follow-through*. Although these fundamentals may be applied in different ways, depending upon whether the rifle is used for plinking, hunting, formal target shooting or home protection, they must always be observed for the most consistent results.

Prior to mastering these fundamentals, the rifle shooter must address two other critical aspects of technique: *hand and eye dominance*, and *grip*.

HAND AND EYE DOMINANCE

Shooting any firearm involves coordination between the eyes and hands. For the majority of people, best shooting is accomplished by firing the gun with the dominant hand and aiming with the dominant eye.

Most people have a *dominant hand*, making them definitely right- or left-handed. Relatively few people are truly *ambidextrous*, or able to perform skills involving manual dexterity equally well with either hand. In most cases, the dominant hand is easily determined, as it is the hand that is used for most one-handed tasks. The dominant hand and arm are often stronger and demonstrate better coordination.

Just as one hand tends to be dominant over the other, the brain also has a preference for one eye over the other, which is known as *eye dominance*. Most often the dominant eye is

Establishing eye dominance: First, focus on a distant object with both eyes open (A). Extend the arms forward with the hands brought together to form a hole between the thumbs, and look at the object through this hole (B). Bring the hands close to the face, still observing the object (C). When the hands are just a few inches from the face, the hole between the hands will be directly in front of the dominant eye.

Chapter 11: Fundamentals of Rifle Shooting

on the same side as the dominant hand, but there are many individuals in whom this is not the case. Many people are not even aware that they have a dominant eye, as in almost all normal activities, both eyes act in concert, and there are few if any normal activities in which one eye only is used. Eye dominance is important in shooting, however, as only one eye is used to aim.

Determining eye dominance is easily accomplished through the following exercise. With both eyes open, focus on a small object at some distance (at least 10-12 feet away). Then extend both hands forward at arm's length, bring the hands together to form a small hole between the webs of the thumbs, and look at the distant object through this hole. Slowly bring the hands to the face, keeping the object in view through the hole between the hands. When the hands are only a few inches from the face, they will be in front of one eye or the other. That eye is the dominant eye. Alternatively, this exercise may be done using a shooting partner, coach or firearm instructor to observe which eye is dominant.

A certain percentage of the population is *cross-dominant*. That is, the dominant hand and dominant eye are on different sides of the body. In virtually all cases, such persons should aim with the dominant eye, and shoulder the gun on that same side. Cross-dominant persons would thus place the butt of the gun against the non-dominant shoulder and use the non-dominant hand to grasp the stock wrist and pull the trigger.

GRIP

There are many shooting positions which may be used for firing a rifle, some of which are specific to certain shooting disciplines. Even before you are introduced to any shooting positions, you must know how to hold the rifle properly. Proper rifle positioning involves the *placement of the buttstock on the shoulder*, the *grip of the firing hand on the small of the stock or pistol grip*, the *placement of the trigger finger on the trigger*, the *placement of the face on the comb*, and the *grip of the support hand on the fore-end*.

The gun butt should be positioned against the shoulder so that you can look through the sights or scope comfortably and naturally with your dominant eye. The buttpad or buttplate should be located in the pocket of the shoulder, the slight crease or depression

 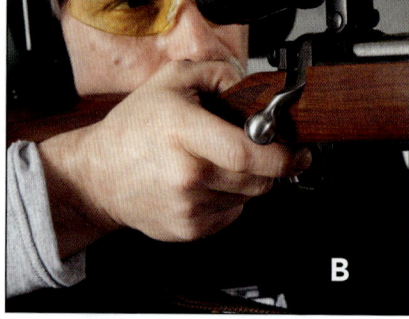

Elements of a proper grip on the rifle: buttstock placement in the pocket of the shoulder. (A); position of firing hand, grasping the stock with the lower three fingers and the thumb resting on top of the stock (B); and position of trigger finger on trigger with contact between the first joint and the tip.

The trigger finger should be clear of the stock.

between the deltoid muscles of the shoulder and the pectoral muscles of the chest. Elevating the firing-hand elbow a bit as the buttstock is placed against the shoulder often helps locate the gun in the pocket. Avoid placing the butt too far out on the deltoid or biceps muscles, or too high, pressing against the collarbone. Proper gun placement against the shoulder helps minimize the discomfort of heavy rifle recoil. Also important is consistency of both the placement of the buttstock and the pressure of the gun against the shoulder. Inconsistency in either of these factors will impair accurate shooting.

Your firing hand should grip the stock firmly with the lower three fingers, and your thumb lightly resting on the top of the stock wrist. Stocks vary in shape, from straight stocks on older lever-action rifles to nearly vertical pistol grips on many target rifles, so your exact firing-hand position may vary somewhat.

Position your hand so that your index finger contacts the trigger between the tip and first joint, and you can pull the trigger straight to the rear. Your trigger finger should be clear of the stock and trigger guard so it will not move the rifle while pulling the trigger.

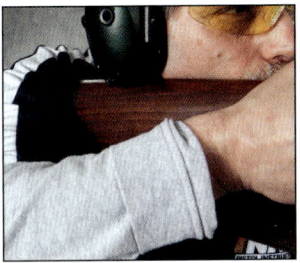

Proper placement of the face on the stock

Placement of your face on the comb will depend upon the height of the comb, the height of the sights, and your own body proportions. Avoid excessive pressure of your cheek or jaw against the stock. Consistency of contact is the key to accurate shooting.

Your support hand should grasp the rifle with just enough pressure to control the rifle under recoil. Too much tension in the supporting arm will tend to throw shots unpredictably. With light-recoiling guns, such as smallbore rifles, the grip of the non-firing hand on the fore-end grip can be quite light, just enough to vertically support the gun. Avoid gripping the fore-end too far out or too close to the body. As with other elements of the grip, consistency in hand placement, grip pressure and muscle tension is most important.

Placement of the support hand on the fore-end

AIMING

Aiming is the process of aligning the barrel with a target so that a bullet fired from the rifle will strike the target where desired. In other words, the point of aim will coincide with the point of impact. Aiming is accomplished using the gun's sights. The most basic and traditional type of sights for rifles are *iron sights*. These can take any of several forms: buckhorn, express, post-and notch, and aperture (see Chapter 12: The Benchrest Position).

Aiming consists of two stages: *sight alignment* and *sight picture*. Sight alignment refers to the proper positioning of the shooting eye, the rear sight, and the front sight in relation

Chapter 11: Fundamentals of Rifle Shooting

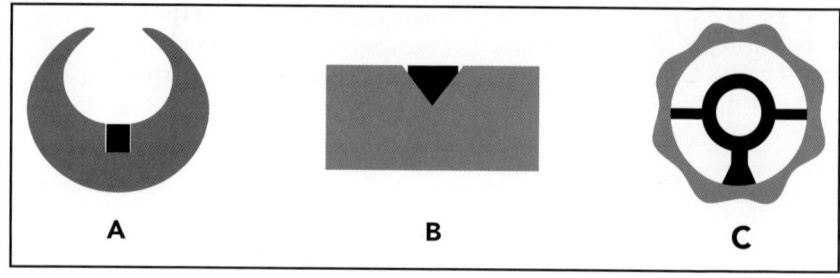

Proper sight alignment varies with the type of iron sight: buckhorn (A), post-and-notch (B), and aperture (C).

to each other. Proper sight alignment depends upon the type of sight used. The accompanying illustrations show proper sight alignment with different types of rifle iron sights.

Sight picture refers to the relationship between the gun's properly aligned sights and the target. This relationship will vary, depending upon the type of sights and the rifle shooting activity in which you are engaged. For example, in traditional bullseye target shooting, post-and-notch iron sights are aligned at the 6 o'clock position in relation to the round black bull, while with aperture sights consisting of a rear peep and front ring, the bullseye is centered in both sights. In other target sports, such as Cowboy Action, practical rifle and three-gun shooting, the aligned sights are typically placed at the center of the target. In hunting, the proper sight picture depends upon the vital area of the game being hunted. And for defensive shooting purposes, the rifle's aligned sights are placed on the center of exposed mass of the target. That is, the sights are placed in the middle of the target area that is exposed.

Telescopic and red-dot sights eliminate concerns about sight alignment, as the aiming reticle and the target are in the same focal plane. The aiming point on the reticle should be centered in the field of view. Proper sight picture with such sights is achieved by putting the crosshairs or dot exactly at the spot on the target where a hit is desired.

Visual focus with iron rifle sights should be on the front sight. This will often make both the rear sight and the target somewhat blurry, but in almost all situations sufficiently clear for good sight alignment and proper sight picture. Those who have difficulty in achieving adequate focus with iron sights may take advantage of an adjustable aperture disk that attaches to the shooting glasses, and sharpens focus on the sights and target.

BREATH CONTROL

Breath control is the method used to minimize gun movement due to breathing. With each breath, your rib cage expands and your shoulders rise slightly. This movement is transmitted to your arms, causing your rifle to shift position in relation to the target.

In rifle activities involving a deliberate and unhurried pace of shooting, breath control is achieved by simply taking a few normal breaths, exhaling, and then stopping your breathing at the natural pause before inhaling. You should hold your breath for only the few seconds required to fire the shot. Typically, maximum steadiness is achieved within about three to eight seconds after breathing has stopped; the shot should thus be fired within that time period. After the shot is fired, you should relax, resume breathing and start the process over again.

In any situation in which you may need to fire a shot quickly, under mental or physical stress, the heart will be pounding and the lungs will be demanding air. Breath control under these circumstances involves simply stopping breathing and holding it. Breathing should simply cease momentarily while the shot is being fired. This will steady the position and allow for a quick shot or series of shots.

HOLD CONTROL

Maximum accuracy is achieved when the firearm is held as still as possible during the process of aiming and firing. *Hold control* is the method by which both the body and the gun are held as still as possible during the period of time when the shot is fired.

Hold control is achieved primarily through a proper grip on the rifle, and a well-balanced, stable shooting position that is naturally aligned with the target, as well as extensive practice. Physical fitness and good muscle tone also contribute to a steady hold. Some positions allow a more stable hold than others. More information on positions and on target alignment is found in the upcoming chapters.

Some novice shooters make the mistake of firing a string of shots without pausing for rest. The first two or three shots may be accurate, but by the fifth or sixth shot, muscle fatigue sets in, impairing good shooting. This is particularly a problem with positions, such as the standing position, in which the rifle is largely supported by the muscles. Until the muscles that support the rifle are strengthened, the shooter should fire only a few shots, and then rest.

TRIGGER CONTROL

Trigger control is one of the most important shooting fundamentals. The term refers to the technique of pulling the trigger without causing any movement of the aligned sights.

Proper trigger control is achieved by applying gradually increasing pressure to the trigger until the shot is fired. This pressure is applied in a rearward direction, not to the side or up or down. The goal of this technique is to produce a "surprise break," in which the shooter cannot predict the exact moment at which the gun will fire.

A surprise break is desired to prevent the shooter from anticipating the shot. New shooters are not accustomed to the recoil, flash and blast that occur when a gun is fired, and thus are prone to reacting more or less instinctively by tightening their muscles, shutting their eyes, and making movements that attempt to counteract the gun's recoil. These involuntary movements are collectively called *flinching* or *anticipating the shot,* and have a negative effect on accuracy by disturbing sight alignment and sight picture just before the shot is fired.

Proper trigger-finger placement

Even in a shooting situation in which a slow, gradual pull may not be possible, such as during a hunt, certain types of competition, or a defensive encounter, trigger control should still be practiced. In such situations, trigger control involves speeding up the process of squeezing the trigger without jerking or flinching. The smoother the trigger is

Chapter 11: Fundamentals of Rifle Shooting

pulled, the less the gun's sights will be disturbed during the firing process, even when the time period is compressed.

As mentioned previously, good trigger control also involves the proper placement of the trigger finger on the trigger, so that the force of the pull to be directed straight to the rear, minimizing a tendency to jerk the gun to the right or left. Proper placement also allows the gun to be fired by moving only the trigger finger.

FOLLOW-THROUGH

The concept of *follow-through* is common to many sports, such as golf, tennis, baseball, bowling and archery. In shooting, follow-through is the effort made by the shooter to integrate, maintain and continue all shooting fundamentals before, during and immediately after firing the shot.

It is true that any alteration in the gun position, stance, sight alignment, and so forth that occurs after the bullet has left the muzzle has no effect whatsoever on accuracy or shot placement. Nonetheless, it is important to consciously maintain the shooting fundamentals for a brief time after the shot has been fired because only by doing so will you be absolutely certain that those fundamentals are applied before and during the firing of the shot. Thus, proper follow-through minimizes gun movement as the shot is fired. A shooter who fails to follow through and applies the fundamentals only up to the breaking of the trigger will (in anticipation of the shot) sooner or later abandon one or more of the fundamentals just prior to firing, resulting in poor shooting.

Proper follow-through does more than just ensure adherence to the shooting fundamentals through the firing of the shot. Follow-through also sets up any successive shots, whenever a shooter may be called upon to fire multiple times accurately and rapidly. The follow-through used in these situations is highly compressed to last only a fraction of a second, but still allows the shooter to maintain a position in alignment with the target and to quickly recover the proper sight picture.

After follow-through, the trigger finger pressure is relaxed, allowing the trigger to reset. However, the trigger finger still maintains contact with the trigger face.

All of the fundamentals of rifle shooting are integrated in the firing of a shot, no matter what the target. The shooter aims (maintaining both sight alignment and the proper sight picture) while momentarily stopping respiration (breath control) and movement (hold control). Only the trigger finger, properly placed, is moved to fire the shot (trigger control). Before, during and after the shot is fired, the shooter observes all the proper shooting fundamentals (follow-through).

CHAPTER 12
Fundamentals of Rifle Shooting Positions

As presented in the previous chapter, the fundamentals of rifle marksmanship are observed regardless of the type of shooting being performed. Effective shooting takes more than just adherence to these fundamentals, however. An effective *shooting position* is the platform from which the fundamentals are applied.

ELEMENTS OF A SHOOTING POSITION

Although there are many effective shooting positions for different situations, all share a number of common characteristics: *consistency, balance, support, natural point of aim* and *comfort*.

CONSISTENCY

Consistency is critical because variations in position produce variations in impact point and/or group size. You must strive to assume each position in the same exact way every time.

In the training phase, this is accomplished by conscious attention to each aspect of the position and each step taken to assume it. With repetition, this process of developing a position "by the numbers" will become ingrained in your subconscious, eventually enabling you to flow into the position quickly, effortlessly, naturally and consistently. The "muscle memory" thus developed through rigorous practice will allow the position to be assumed easily and automatically.

BALANCE

Balance is also an essential component of a proper firing position. Whatever position you are in—benchrest, standing, kneeling, sitting or prone—the most stable shooting platform is achieved with the body weight evenly distributed and a neutral posture. A balanced position absorbs recoil and facilitates reacquisition of the sights and accurate follow-up shots.

Keeping your head erect and level also is important. The brain senses body position by a number of mechanisms, including a structure in the inner ear known as the labyrinth. Moreover, visual inputs from the eyes provide important feedback to the brain to help maintain balance. An upright, level head position

A balanced shooting position

maximizes the ability of both the the labyrinth and the eyes to promote body equilibrium and efficient body movement.

SUPPORT

A good position also offers *support* to minimize gun movement while aiming. Support can be provided by the skeleton, muscle tension or an external object, such as sandbags on a bench.

Also, the position should provide maximum *bone support*. This means that, as much as possible, you should use bones rather than muscles to support the body and the rifle. If you rely primarily on muscles to support the weight of the rifle, you will have a hard time relaxing and keeping the rifle steady.

Different positions allow different levels of bone support. The least support is offered by the free arm standing position, while the greatest is offered by the sitting and prone positions.

A proper shooting position makes use of bone support for stability.

Additional support may be achieved by using a rifle sling (see Appendix A, Using the Sling) or by utilizing objects in the environment to help support the rifle. For example, when hunting, additional support may be provided by stumps, rocks, tree trunks and branches and the like. Also, in certain types of rifle competition, it is permissible to use artificial support (such as bipods, tripod rests and sandbags) in some events.

NATURAL POINT OF AIM (NPA)

A proper firing position is naturally aligned with the target. Each shooter has a natural point of aim (NPA) unique to his or her body in every position.

To determine your NPA, first assume your position, with your eyes open and your gun aimed at a target. Next, close your eyes. With your eyes still closed, relax and find the body position that feels most natural. In some positions it may be helpful to make a circle with the rifle, and then settle into the position. Then, open your eyes and observe where your gun's sights are pointed in relation to the target. Ideally, the sight picture will be aligned with the target. If the sight picture is aligned to the right or left or slightly high or low, you will have to modify some aspect of the position (such as foot placement in the standing position, or the angle of the body on the ground for the prone position) to achieve the proper natural alignment.

Of course, except when shooting off sandbags, the sight picture does not stay perfectly still, as it is impossible to hold a rifle without some movement. When proper NPA is achieved, the "wobble area" of the sights will be centered on the target.

Repeat the NPA exercise until your position is adjusted for the proper natural alignment. You should make every effort to put yourself in this same alignment each time the

In the NPA (Natural Point of Aim) exercise, the shooter first assumes a position with the gun aimed at a target (A). Then the eyes are closed, and the gun moved in an arc or circle (B) until it comes to rest in the position that feels most naturally stable and comfortable. The eyes are then opened (C) and the shooter observes where the rifle's sights are in relation to the target. If the "wobble area" of the sights is not centered on the target, the shooter's position should be modified to achieve the proper sight picture while taking advantage of the body's natural alignment.

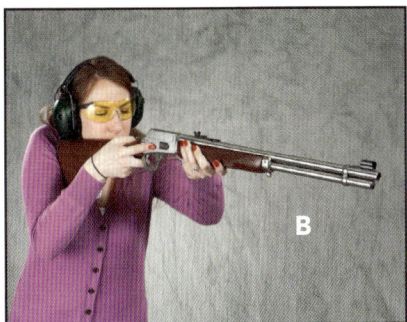

position is assumed in order to take advantage of your NPA. Also, periodically repeat the NPA exercise, as changes in shooting experience, posture, age and so forth can affect the body's natural alignment.

COMFORT

Finally, a proper position should be *comfortable*. A stance that is not comfortable—one that is forced, awkward, strained or painful—is unlikely to be consistent or stable, and thus will not contribute to effective shooting. When practicing shooting positions, you should be conscious of how natural and comfortable each position is. Positions that do not feel comfortable must be modified as necessary. However, in some cases discomfort may be the result of the lack of joint flexibility or muscular strength. In such cases, a minimal amount of physical training is usually all that is needed to allow the shooter to comfortably assume a proper shooting position. Of course, any shooter should consult his or her doctor prior to starting any physical training regimen.

LEARNING A SHOOTING POSITION

The rifle shooter may have the need to learn only one or two, or several, shooting positions. Whether the position is simple or complex, the process for mastering it is the same, and involves a specific series of steps.

The first step in learning a shooting position is to *study the position*. This means knowing what is involved in the position, how it is assumed, and the purpose of the position.

The second step is to *practice the position without a rifle*. Just about every shooting position places special demands upon the shooter in terms of balance, coordination, hand and foot placement, and more. Practicing these aspects of the position without a rifle simplifies the position, breaking the learning process into a number of steps that build upon each other.

Next, *practice the position with an unloaded rifle*. Any shooting position can effectively be practiced using an empty gun in the dry-fire mode, with care taken to observe all dry-firing safety rules (see Chapter 18: Additional Opportunities for Skill Development).

During dry-fire practice, *align the position with the target*. Each shooter will have a different alignment with the target for each shooting position. Perform the Natural Point of Aim (NPA) exercise described earlier in this chapter with every shooting position learned.

Once the position has been acquired using an empty gun, *test the position* with live ammunition. Live-fire testing will reveal if there are aspects of the position, or the shooting fundamentals, that need to be corrected.

After the skills presented in this chapter have been mastered, proceed to learning the various shooting positions. The positions taught in the NRA Basic Rifle Shooting Course are the benchrest and standing positions. The prone, kneeling and sitting positions are also presented in this book. These positions, presented in succeeding chapters, should suffice for the great majority of shooting activities in which the novice will take part.

CHAPTER 13
The Benchrest Position

The most fundamental position that any new rifle shooter should learn is the benchrest position. The position derives its name from the fact that the shooter fires from a seated position, using one or more rests on a shooting bench for rifle support.

PREPARING TO USE THE BENCHREST POSITION

Before assuming the benchrest position, a number of items must be assembled. First and foremost is a *shooting bench* approximately 30"-36" high, with sufficient space for the shooter's elbows, sandbag rests, ammunition and spotting scope, if used. Sturdiness and stability are a must; card tables, planks across sawhorses, etc. do not afford the steady rest necessary for accurate shooting. Best are benches designed expressly for shooters; some may have a cutout for the shooter's upper body.

The next requirement is a *chair* or *stool* for use with the shooting bench. This should be high enough so that about half of the shooter's torso is above the bench. Proper height in relation to the shooter's legs is also important. The seat should allow the shooter's feet to be flat on the ground, with an angle at the knee joint of approximately 90 degrees. The exact angle will vary somewhat, depending upon the leg length of the shooter.

Also needed is a *rest* or *rests* for supporting the rifle. Most often a front rest is used to support the fore-end, and a rear rest is used under the buttstock.

Proper benchrest technique: head erect, back straight, feet solidly on the ground, rifle properly supported and pulled into the shoulder.

There are many types of front rests, from simple sandbags to precision tripod rests. These latter units have a small sandbag mounted on a heavy three-legged base; and feature adjustments for height and, sometimes, windage.

Virtually all rear rests are variations on a sandbag design. Some specialized units for competition have extra-heavy bases and ears proportioned to precisely hold the buttstock.

Hard-kicking rifles tend to lift the shooting hand and, as a consequence, drive the elbow of the shooting arm downward. Thus, for extended benchrest sessions with heavy-recoiling centerfire rifles, an *elbow pad* is often recommended.

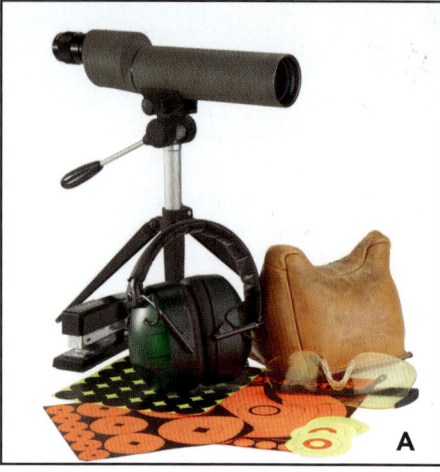

Some of the accessories useful for benchrest shooting: Spotting scope, hearing protection, eye protection, stapler and target posters (A). Different types of rifle rests: rear sandbag (B), front rest (C), bipod (D).

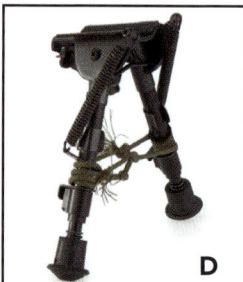

Other accessories for benchrest shooting include a *pad* for the elbow of the shooting arm; a *spotting scope* for seeing bullet holes in distant targets; a supply of *targets* and *target pasters*; a *stapler* for affixing the targets to a target board or backer; and of course, eye and hearing protection. More information on useful shooting accessories is found in Chapter 19: Selecting Rifles, Ammunition and Accessories.

ASSUMING THE BENCHREST POSITION

Before assuming the benchrest position, assure that the bench and shooting stool are situated on level ground, and do not rock or wobble. Sit at the bench with the chair or stool positioned so as to allow a comfortable, upright position with your feet flat on the ground and your body weight equally distributed. Your upper body should be near the bench top, but not touching it.

Next, use the unloaded rifle to try different rest positions to find the one offering the greatest stability, balance, and comfort. Rest height is of considerable importance, as the proper height places the buttstock squarely in the pocket of your shoulder, and allows your head to be in a natural upright position in which you can see the sights out of the center of the dominant eye. If you have to lean forward or drop your head excessively to see the gun's sights, the rest height should be increased.

The front sandbag, tripod rest or other rest device should be placed around 3"-5" back of the tip of the fore-end (slightly further forward with rifles having long, heavy barrels). The rest should allow the gun to slide freely in recoil, but also provide lateral stability. Avoid interference of sling swivels or sling swivel studs with the front rest.

A special type of front support is the *bipod*. This device attaches to the underside of the

Proper position of a rear sandbag (A); A bipod (B) is an alternative to a front sandbag.

fore-end and features two legs that angle out to either side to provide stability. The legs of most units are adjustable for length.

The rear sandbag should be placed under the buttstock just forward of the stock toe. Again, avoid interference of rear sling swivels or studs with the bag. Since most rifles have an angled stock belly, bag placement can be used to adjust vertical sight picture.

Some shooters forgo a rear sandbag, and support the buttstock with the non-shooting hand. This method does not generally provide the consistent and precise support of a rear bag.

Variations on the benchrest position: using the support hand under the buttstock instead of a rear sandbag (A) and holding the fore-end of a rifle with the support hand (B).

In the most common variant of the benchrest position, your shoulders will be at an angle to the target, with the gun firmly into the pocket of your firing-hand shoulder. Consistent shoulder pressure on the buttpad is one of the keys to accurate benchrest shooting. Your support-hand elbow will rest on the bench and the support hand either supports the buttstock or squeezes the rear bag to make minor elevation changes during aiming. Alternatively, with heavy-recoiling rifles, it may be necessary for your support hand to grip the fore-end, to prevent the rifle from coming off the rest. Use light to moderate force in gripping the stock with your firing hand, and avoid applying lateral pressure to the stock. Your trigger finger should exert force directly rearward, in line with the axis of the bore.

Once you have obtained a comfortable, stable and balanced position, with the rifle properly supported, dry-fire the rifle to verify the position. A proper benchrest position will allow you to dry-fire the rifle with no movement of the sights.

After successfully dry-firing, you may proceed to live ammunition. Recoil may require minor modifications of the position. In general, the most accurate benchrest shooting is done with relaxed hands and arms, and a light grip.

USING THE BENCHREST POSITION TO ZERO THE RIFLE

One of the first tasks any new gun owner must do is to zero the firearm. *Zeroing* involves making the rifle's sights and point of impact coincide, with a particular brand of ammunition at a given distance. The benchrest position is ideal for rifle zeroing because it is the position that affords the greatest accuracy, allowing higher confidence in the observed changes in bullet impact that occur with sight adjustments.

Zeroing an adjustable-sight rifle, or one having a red-dot or telescopic sight, is relatively easy. Use a fairly large target—a 24" by 24" sheet of paper or larger—with a relatively small aiming point, such as a 3" bullseye. With the target placed at 25 yards downrange, fire one to three shots at the bullseye, concentrating on the shooting fundamentals.

All shots fired should impact close together, forming a *shot group*. If the shots do not coincide with the dot used as an aiming point, the sights must be adjusted.

Most commonly with iron sights, both windage and elevation are adjusted using knobs or screws on the rear sight unit. The rear sight is moved in the direction of the desired change in bullet impact. Thus, if the bullet hits below the aiming point, the rear sight must be adjusted so that its blade or aperture sits higher, to raise the location of bullet impact. Similarly, to move bullet impact to the right, the rear sight blade or aperture must be moved to the right. Most adjustable rear sights have an engraved arrow or letter to indicate the direction of adjustment achieved by turning the windage and elevation adjusting screws or knobs in a particular direction.

Many target-style adjustable iron sights have "click adjustments" that give the shooter a tactile click each time the adjusting knob or screw is turned slightly. Each click produces a standard or predictable amount of change in bullet impact at a known distance (e.g., $1/4$" at 100 yards), making precise and repeatable sight adjustments easier.

Some rifles, such as lever-actions for hunting, have a buckhorn style rear sight adjusted by means of a stepped elevator piece that allows only coarse elevation changes. Windage adjustment is achieved by drifting the front sight laterally in its mounting dovetail. It is important to realize that the front sight must be moved in the *opposite* direction you want

Adjusting iron sights (l.) and a telescopic rifle sight (r.)

the shot group to move. Such buckhorn sights lack precision, but are usually adequate for the gun's intended purpose of taking deer-size game at relatively close range (around 125 yards or less).

Red-dot and telescopic sights have similar windage and elevation adjustments, usually by means of knobs or dials that are often located roughly in the middle of the sight. The direction of adjustment, and the value of each click, are normally found on the scope's adjustment knobs or dials. Many click values are given in *minutes of angle* (1 m.o.a.=1.04" at 100 yards). Common click values for rifle scopes are $1/2$" and $1/4$" at 100 yards, or (approximately) $1/2$ and $1/4$ m.o.a. Adjustment instructions and other information are found in each rifle scope's owner's manuals.

Once the point of aim and the bullet impacts coincide at 25 yards, the target may be moved back to 50 or even 100 yards, and the gun zeroed for the new range. This process can be repeated until the gun is zeroed at any distance desired.

Some shooters find it useful to zero the gun at 100 yards, and then rezero for longer ranges, taking note of the number of clicks of elevation required for each of the longer ranges. This allows the gun to be easily returned to its 100-yard zero, as well as the longer-range zeros.

USING THE BENCHREST POSITION TO IMPROVE RIFLE SHOOTING

Many novice rifle owners, when shooting offhand or from various other rifle positions, spend most of their concentration and energy in trying to hold the rifle steady on target, and, as a result, often fail to observe all the shooting fundamentals of aiming, breath control, trigger control and follow-through. The benchrest position, because it eliminates the need to hold the rifle steady, allows the shooter to focus on the fundamentals, and is thus a good tool for refining shooting technique.

Shooting from the benchrest position is not just for beginners, however. Most top competitive shooters regularly spend time shooting groups from the benchrest position. This activity allows them to consciously focus on, and review, individual aspects of technique.

In addition to technique, many other things may influence shooting accuracy, including the ammunition brand and load, gun components such as barrels and triggers, type and magnification of sights, and even accessories such as shooting glasses. The stability and precision of the benchrest position makes it ideal for evaluating the effects of these factors on performance. For the same reason, it is the position most often used to perform accuracy comparisons between different guns. For more information on testing and comparing guns and ammunition, see Chapter 19: Selecting Rifles, Ammunition and Accessories.

CHAPTER 14
The Standing Position

The well-rounded rifle shooter must be comfortable with a variety of positions, not just shooting off the bench or from prone. The standing shooting position is the classic rifle shooting position, and is also useful in many hunting and competition situations. The standing position is natural and intuitive to assume.

There are two variations of the standing shooting position: the *free arm* and the *arm rest* positions. The type of shooting you are doing determines the variation you will use.

ASSUMING THE FREE ARM STANDING SHOOTING POSITION

The free arm position is used when the time available to fire a shot is very short; when the target is moving, such as in hunting situations; or when a number of rounds must be fired quickly, as in the NRA America's Rifle Challenge matches and similar competition. Shooters who use this position should be sure that they have sufficient arm strength to comfortably support the rifle, or a rifle light enough for their level of strength.

To assume the free arm standing position, first face the target with the rifle in both hands. Turn the body nearly 90 degrees toward the shooting-hand side (to the right if you pull the trigger with your right index finger, and to the left if you use your left index finger). The feet should be about shoulder width apart, with the body weight distributed equally on both feet.

Raise the rifle to eye level and place the buttstock firmly into the pocket of the firing-hand shoulder. The support hand should be about halfway out on the fore-end, supporting the weight of the rifle, and, as much as possible, the support-hand elbow should be directly below the gun and not angled out

Free-arm standing shooting position: A. Hunting B. Defensive

to the side. The firing hand grips the wrist of the stock firmly. The body should be upright and not leaning backward, and the head should be erect (although that will depend somewhat on the height of the sights and the body configuration of the shooter). When shooting a heavy-recoiling rifle, or firing a quick sequence of shots, you may wish to lean forward slightly, "into the shot," for better control.

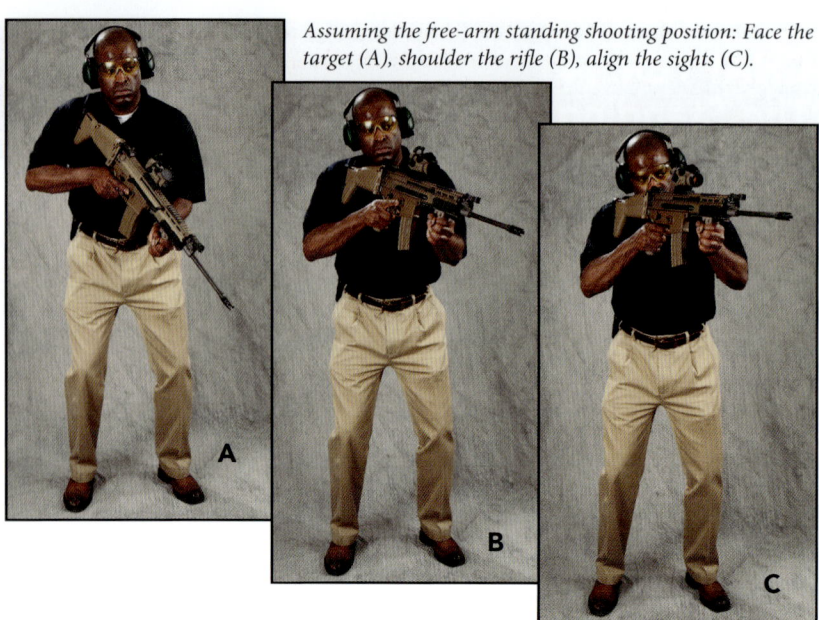

Assuming the free-arm standing shooting position: Face the target (A), shoulder the rifle (B), align the sights (C).

Finally, the position must be aligned with the target. Vertical alignment is achieved simply by raising or lowering the muzzle of the rifle, while horizontal alignment is made by moving the feet. Avoid "muscling the gun" into alignment; use the Natural Point Of Aim exercise described in Chapter 11 to put the natural body position into proper target alignment.

ASSUMING THE ARM REST STANDING SHOOTING POSITION

The arm rest standing position is used when a higher degree of stability and accuracy are required, and time is not as critical, such as in most target events. Not only is the arm rest position steadier than the free arm position; it also often allows a shooter to use a rifle that is too heavy to comfortably hold in the free arm position.

To assume the arm rest position, start as before, facing the target with the gun held in both hands, and then turn approximately 90 degrees toward the firing hand. Your feet are shoulder width apart, your body weight is evenly distributed on your feet, and your head is erect.

The arm-rest standing shooting position

Raise the rifle to eye level, and place the butt into the pocket of the shoulder. As in the free arm position, support the rifle's weight with the non-firing hand, but lean your upper body away from the target, and bend your support arm so the upper portion of your arm rests on your side or hip. The support hand wrist is straight and the hand is not placed far out on the fore-end, but closer to your body, under the action. In a proper position, your support-hand forearm is nearly vertical.

As with the free arm position, vertical alignment of the sights and target is achieved simply by raising or lowering the muzzle, usually by moving the position of the support hand on the fore-end. Moving the support hand inward, or closer to the trigger guard, will tend to raise the muzzle, while extending the support hand further forward will lower the muzzle. Horizontal alignment is achieved by moving the feet. Spreading the feet apart or bringing them closer together may also change vertical sight alignment. The Natural Point Of Aim exercise will help you achieve a comfortable, naturally aligned position.

A variety of support-hand positions may be used with the arm rest standing position. These different positions allow for variations in the height of the rifle, but in all of them the wrist is still kept straight, for maximum support.

Variations in hand position with the arm rest standing shooting position: These positions accommodate different rifle heights and offer maximum support.

CHAPTER 15
The Prone Position

The prone position is the steadiest of the four positions (standing, kneeling, sitting and prone) used in various NRA and International position shooting events. This position is also employed in long-range and F-Class events, practical rifle shooting, and in hunting situations in the field.

In the prone position, both elbows and almost the entire body are in contact with the ground, maximizing stability. To assume the position, first stand facing the target with the rifle in both hands. With the rifle in your support hand, lower your body to your knees. Keep the rifle pointed in a safe direction at all times.

Next, with the rifle still in your support hand, extend your firing hand forward and lower your body to the ground in a controlled manner. Your body should not be aligned straight with the target, but should be angled slightly away from your firing-hand side, with the legs extended slightly out to the sides for stability. Extend the support-hand elbow forward. Finally, bring your firing hand to the rifle and bring the gun to eye level, placing the butt firmly into the shoulder.

The prone position

As much as possible, keep your support-hand elbow directly under your support hand and the rifle. This maximizes bone support and minimizes the muscle tension required to hold the gun.

There are two ways of placing your body in the prone position. In the *flat prone* position, your body lies flat, and the gun is held fairly low to the ground. In the *rollover prone* position, once your body is properly angled away from your firing-hand side, roll your torso toward the support-hand side. Finally, pull up your knee on the firing-hand side. The rollover prone position is preferred by some because it takes pressure off the rib cage and abdomen and makes breathing easier. Also, the head and gun are slightly higher than

Chapter 15: The Prone Position   89

Assuming the prone position: First, face the target with the rifle in both hands (A). With the rifle in the shooting hand, lower your body to your knees (B). Extend your firing hand forward (C) and lower your body fully to the ground (D). Extend your support arm forward (E) and bring the rifle to eye level and place the butt of the gun firmly into the shoulder (F).

Flat prone (A) and rollover prone (B) positions, seen from the rear. Note the flat feet in the flat prone position. Also note the torso rolled toward the support-hand side, and the firing-side knee drawn up, in rollover prone.

in the flat prone position. However, some shooters find the rollover prone position awkward or tiring, as it puts more weight on the support elbow.

Try to achieve a consistent and relaxed foot placement in the prone position. In the flat prone position, your feet should be almost flat on the ground, with the toes angled out laterally. In the rollover prone position, your feet may be again flat on the ground, or you may also cross your firing-side foot over the support-side foot.

To adjust rifle position vertically in the prone position, move your support hand in or out on the fore-end. Pulling the support hand to the rear will raise the gun's muzzle, while extending it forward lowers the muzzle. To adjust the position horizontally, rotate the entire position around the support-hand elbow. As with all positions, it is essential to find and use your prone position natural point of aim to ensure that you are naturally aligned with the target. Avoid the temptation to "muscle" the rifle into alignment with the target.

The steadiness of the position may be increased through the use of a sling (see Appendix A: Using the Sling), a bipod, or any available support in the field, such as a downed tree trunk or even a rolled-up jacket or knapsack.

Additional support in the prone position may be achieved by using a sling.

Chapter 15: The Prone Position

CHAPTER 16
The Kneeling Position

The kneeling position is one of the positions used in both high power and smallbore position shooting (see Chapter 17: Rifle Shooting Activities). Other rifle shooting disciplines, such as the NRA America's Rifle Challenge, practical rifle shooting, and even Cowboy Action Shooting make use of the kneeling position in their events.

The kneeling position is also highly useful in the field, as it is quick to assume, steadier than the standing position and provides the clearance to shoot over brush, obstacles or uneven terrain. Finally, in home defense situations, it may be necessary to fire from behind a low barricade; the kneeling position is ideal for this.

To assume the kneeling position, stand facing the target with the rifle grasped in both hands. Turn away from the target around 30 to 45 degrees toward the firing-hand (dominant-eye) side. Drop down to your knee on that side, and sit on your foot. Be sure to control the muzzle and keep the rifle pointed in a safe direction during this movement.

Adjust the position of your support-side foot so that your lower leg on that side is vertical. Place your support-arm elbow on your knee and raise the rifle to eye level, bringing the rifle butt into your shoulder.

To achieve the best bone support, place your support arm directly above your knee on that side, so that the weight of your arm and the gun is directed straight down through your elbow to your knee and lower leg. Avoid canting the gun inward or outward in relation to your support-arm elbow.

Also avoid leaning too far forward or backward. Your position should be balanced between the front and rear feet, with a slight forward lean of your upper body to counteract recoil. If your head is thrust too far forward or down, raise the position of the rifle by moving your support hand rearward on the fore-end.

There are two ways to sit on the foot on the firing-hand side. The most popular method is to bend your foot forward at the toes, keeping the sole of your shoe-tip on the ground. Your body will rest on the back of the heel. The second method is to extend your foot straight and fully rearward so that the top of your foot, and not the sole, is in contact with the ground. This second foot position places the body closer to the ground, and is thus potentially more stable, but is difficult for many people to assume because of the flexibility it requires. Most competitive shooters also take advantage of a *kneeling roll*, a cylindrical cushion placed under the rear ankle for support and comfort.

The kneeling position

Assuming the kneeling position: First, face the target with the rifle in both hands (A). Turn toward the firing-hand side (B) and drop to that knee, sitting on the foot (C). Keep the rifle pointed in a safe direction during this movement. Move the support-side foot so that the lower leg on that side is vertical and place the support-arm elbow on the knee (D). Finally, bring the rifle to eye level and place the butt of the gun firmly into the shoulder (E).

The foot in the kneeling position may be in the high (left) or low (below) positions. A kneeling roll (bottom left) may also be used for support.

Adjusting the vertical position of the rifle is achieved by moving your support hand further forward or rearward on the fore-end. Horizontal position is adjusted by rotating your position around the firing-hand knee on the ground.

Additional support in the kneeling position can be achieved by using a sling (see Appendix A: Using the Sling). In the field, there are numerous methods to increase the steadiness of the position. Rifle support may be enhanced by resting your rifle on a tree branch, stump, or fence, or by leaning your body against a tree trunk or other solid object.

Chapter 16: The Kneeling Position

CHAPTER 17
The Sitting Position

The sitting position is one of the steadiest rifle shooting positions discussed in this book. The sitting position is employed in NRA position shooting, and is also useful in hunting situations in the field.

The main benefit of the sitting position is its stability, which is the result of good bone support. In a proper sitting position, both elbows rest on the knees, and relatively little muscle tension is used to hold the position or support the gun. Like the kneeling position, the sitting position provides better ground clearance than the prone position. However, it takes more time to assume than the kneeling position.

To assume the sitting position, stand facing the target with the rifle in both hands. Turn your body about 30 to 45 degrees toward the firing-hand side, and, with the rifle in the support hand, sit down on the ground or floor. Be sure to maintain the rifle in a safe direction at all times.

The sitting position.

Next, extend your legs partially forward, and cross your support-side ankle over the other. This will leave the knees somewhat elevated. Place both elbows just forward of your kneecaps, so that each arm contacts the knee joint just behind the elbow. Raise the rifle to eye level and bring the butt firmly into the shoulder.

As much as possible, keep the rifle directly above the wrist, elbow and knee on the support-hand side; this will direct the rifle's weight

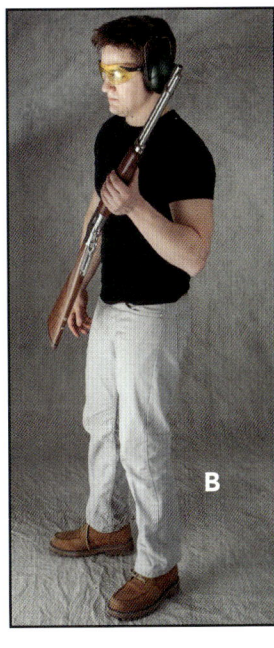

Assuming the sitting position: First, face the target with the rifle in both hands (A). Turn away from the target toward your firing-hand side (B).

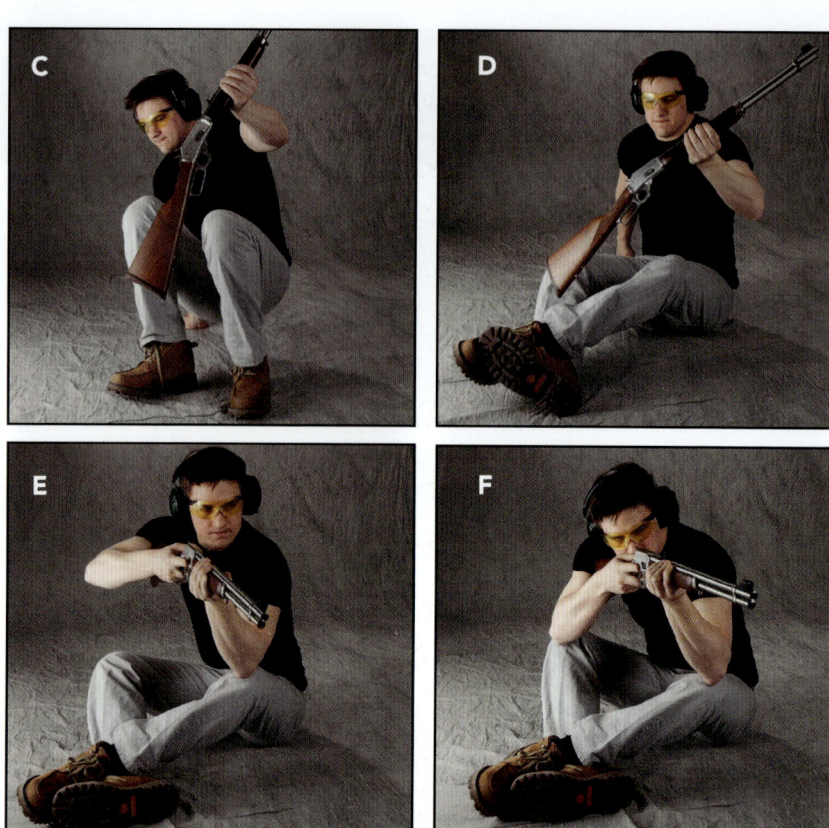

Assuming the sitting position (continued): With the rifle in the support hand, sit on the ground (C). Extend the legs forward and cross the support-side ankle over the ankle on the firing-hand side (D). Place your elbows forward of your knees (E), bring the rifle to eye level and place the butt of the gun firmly into the shoulder (F).

downward primarily against bones and joint, rather than muscles. Avoid canting the gun outward or inward.

    Rather than extend both legs forward in front of the body, shooters in the sitting position often bring them inward, bringing the feet under the knees and crossing the ankles in a position similar to that of a yoga pose. The knees, in this position, are somewhat flatter, and rest on top of the feet, and the elbows are placed on the insides of the knees rather than on top of them. This variation provides great stability and rigidity, and good recoil control for rapid-fire target shooting or quick follow-up shots on game in the field. However, this version of the sitting position requires somewhat more flexibility than the first variant described in this chapter.

    Whichever version of the sitting position is used, vertical adjustment of the rifle is accomplished by moving your support hand outward on the fore-end (to lower the rifle) or bringing that hand inward (to raise the rifle). Horizontal adjustment is achieved simply by rotating the position around the buttocks. As with all positions, you should establish your Natural Point of Aim for this position, and practice getting into position with your body properly and naturally aligned with the target until it is second nature. This will ensure that you will assume a properly-aligned position in the field or on the firing line without having to consciously think about it, or without spending time readjusting the position.

The steadiness of the sitting position may be increased through the use of a sling (see Appendix A: Using the Sling), a bipod, cross-sticks, or any available supporting object in the field, such as a fence, tree stump, or branch.

PART IV

RIFLE SHOOTING ACTIVITIES

CHAPTER 18
Rifle Shooting Activities

In general, there are four main uses for a firearm: *recreational shooting*, *hunting*, *target competition*, and *home protection*. Despite claims to the contrary by those seeking to further restrict their ownership, rifles are commonly employed for all of these activities.

RECREATIONAL SHOOTING

Although many thousands of shooters own rifles for hunting, for formal target shooting, or for self-defense, by far the greatest number of shots fired from rifles each year involve casual recreational shooting, often called *plinking*. Plinking is simply the name given to any form of informal target shooting, done with any type of rifle at any type of safe target. The only limitations placed on this activity are those imposed by safety, legal restrictions, and the shooter's imagination.

Plinking is often done at a dedicated indoor or outdoor range facility. Shooting ranges can usually be found by looking on the internet, or by asking a local gun shop. Each range will have rules dealing with safety, permissible shooting positions, caliber restrictions and so forth. Some ranges may have a Range Safety Officer on duty. Every shooter is responsible for learning and observing all range rules.

Recreational shooting, or "plinking," is the name given to any safe, legal informal target shooting.

Some shooters may prefer to shoot on public or private land rather than a formal range (subject to applicable local, state and federal laws). In such situations, however, safety is even more of a concern. The shooter must be responsible for always pointing the rifle in a safe direction, establishing a proper backstop, ensuring that unauthorized persons do not wander into the line of fire and so forth. The safety rule "Know Your Target and What is Beyond" is particularly important in such situations, as a bullet from even a .22 rimfire may travel a mile or more from a rifle fired when pointing skyward. Shooters must also be good stewards of the land, not trespassing on private property, removing all their spent cases and trash, and avoiding improper targets, such as glass bottles, old batteries, etc.

Rifle owners may use recreational shooting to sharpen their skills for hunting, target shooting or home protection; most often, however, the emphasis is simply on fun. While standard bullseye targets are extremely popular, other types of targets—many in vogue decades ago—including those consisting of small dots (used for "dot shooting"), playing card decks (used to shoot poker hands), arrays of letters or numbers, and so forth. In the absence of a printed target, challenges may be improvised. For example, a piece of 8 $^1/_2$" by 11" piece of paper may be put out at 25 to 50 yards, and a single bullet hole put somewhere on the sheet. Each successive shooter must attempt to place his or her shot as close as possible to the original bullet hole.

In addition to a gun and ammunition, recreational shooting usually requires additional gear, such as a rifle case, shooting bag, cleaning kit, tool kit and, of course, eye and ear protection.

Finally, recreational shooting is the best way to introduce a new shooter to rifle shooting, and to ingrain the rules of safety and the principles of good marksmanship in a relaxed and friendly atmosphere.

RIFLE HUNTING

Hunters probably constitute the largest single group of rifle shooters in America. Rifles are used by millions of hunters each year to take everything from birds and squirrels to big-game such as deer, elk, moose and bear, and even dangerous African game such as lion and Cape buffalo.

There are basically three types of rifle hunting activities: *small game hunting and pest control* (involving game such as squirrels, rabbits and crows), *varmint hunting* (involving game such as prairie dogs, groundhogs and coyotes),

Rifle hunting typically involves skill in stalking, marksmanship and woodsmanship.

and *big-game hunting* (involving deer-sized and larger animals). Each type of hunting involves different types of firearms, ammunition and accessories, as well as different shooting skills.

Some jurisdictions have certain requirements for hunting rifles, such as a minimum caliber for deer or other game of a similar size, or limitations on the capacity of magazines for semi-automatic hunting rifles. Almost all jurisdictions mandate every hunter to have a hunting license, sometimes issued upon successful completion of a hunter education course. Regulations regarding hunting on public or private lands are usually readily available from the state fish and game service or other similar office.

Advice on the selection of rifles, ammunition and accessories for a particular type of hunting can be obtained from a variety of sources, including local gun shops, gun clubs, hunting guides or outfitters, videos and DVDs, books, hunting websites, online forums on the internet, and hunting-oriented magazines such as *The American Hunter*.

TARGET SHOOTING

Many rifle owners participate in various types of target competition, sometimes simply to sharpen their skills for other shooting activities. There are far too many rifle target-shooting sports to discuss all of them here. The vast majority of rifle target shooters compete in *NRA* or *international rifle competition, practical rifle competition, silhouette competition, cowboy action shooting* and *benchrest competition*.

NRA RIFLE COMPETITION

There are two types of NRA rifle competition. *NRA Smallbore* matches are shot with either the *light rifle* or *match rifle*, chambered in a .22 rimfire cartridge. Competition is held at 50 feet, 50 yards/meters, or 100 yards. Courses of fire include three-position (prone, standing and kneeling), four-position (prone, standing, sitting and kneeling) and prone matches. Almost all NRA smallbore competition is fired with iron sights, although telescopic sights are used in some matches.

F-Class shooting can be done using telescopic sights and bipod or tripod rests with sandbags.

NRA High Power competition involves the use of various types of centerfire rifles fired from different shooting positions at bullseye targets set at 100 to 1,000 yards. There are many classes of rifles used in high power competition. Most shooters participate in one of three forms of high power shooting. In *Service rifle* competition, rifles similar to military-issue M1 Garand, M14 or M16 rifles are used. *Match rifle* competition involves the use of heavy, highly specialized bolt-action or semi-automatic rifles having few restrictions. Service rifles and match rifles are usually used for *position shooting* at different ranges. A typical *across-the-course* match consists of slow-fire shooting from standing at a 200-yard target; rapid-fire shooting from sitting or kneeling at 200 yards; rapid-fire

Chapter 18: Rifle Shooting Activities

shooting at 300 yards from prone; and slow-fire shooting from prone at 600 yards.

Palma Rifle competition features long-barreled bolt-action rifles chambered for the .223 Remington or .308 Win. cartridge. These are used in Palma matches, which involve firing from the prone position at targets at 800, 900 and 1,000 yards.

No external support is allowed in any of these types of competition, although a sling and shooting jacket are permitted. Iron sights are required, except in long-range "any sight" matches, where a telescopic sight may be used.

NRA Service Rifle (top), Match Rifle and Smallbore rifle, with accessories.

Additionally, F-Class competition is quite popular. In this sport, all shooting is done from the prone position at targets 300 to 1,000 yards away, and telescopic sights and rests or bipods are allowed. Two classes have been established: the F/TR class, limited to 18.2 pounds, a front bipod, and either a standard .223 Rem. or .308 Win. chambering. F/Open rifles may weigh 22 pounds and utilize a tripod front rest, and can be chambered for any cartridge of .35 caliber or smaller.

INTERNATIONAL RIFLE COMPETITION

International Rifle competition is practiced worldwide, with some events featured in the Olympics. International centerfire rifle competition is conducted at 300 meters, with three events: *300 meter three-position, 300 meter prone,* and *300 meter standard rifle*. Smallbore events include *50 meter three-position* and *50-meter prone* for both men and women. Finally, there are *10 meter air rifle* events, again for both men and women.

Each event is shot with specially designed rifles. Most specialized are the free rifles used in both 300 meter and smallbore competition, which weigh up to 8 kilograms (approximately 17 pounds, 10 ounces) and feature long, heavy match-grade barrels, very light triggers, and ergonomic stocks having adjustable cheekpieces and butt plates. *Smallbore sport rifles* resemble smallbore free rifles, but are limited to 6.5 kilograms (14 pounds, 5 ounces). *Standard rifles*, centerfire rifles used for 300-meter competition, may weigh no more than 5.5 kilograms (12 pounds, 2 ounces) and have additional

Typical rifles used in international competition include free rifles, smallbore sport rifles, 300-meter standard rifles, and air rifles.

restrictions on minimum trigger pull weight, caliber, stock and sight design and allowable accessories. *Air rifles* used in international competition are subject to many of the same restrictions as 300-meter standard rifles, and there are also competitive classes for certain types of NRA High Power rifles.

Typical accessories for all forms of international rifle shooting include a spotting scope and stand, a shooting mat, shooting glasses, and a shooting jacket, hat and gloves.

International rifle events are among the most exacting forms of target shooting, and will provide any shooter with a lifetime of challenge. For more information visit: compete.nra.org

PRACTICAL RIFLE COMPETITION

The various rifle shooting sports known collectively as *practical rifle competition* emphasize speed and accuracy in engaging targets in varied and ever-changing arrays inspired by military, law-enforcement or defensive situations.

Targets are large cardboard silhouettes with embossed scoring rings, or steel plates of various sizes and shapes. Practical rifle events make use of either time limits or *Comstock scoring*, in which both the point value of the hits, as well as the elapsed time to shoot the stage, are used to compute the score. Penalties are assessed for exceeding time limits, missing the target, or hitting "hostage" or "no-shoot" targets.

There are two types of practical rifle competition widely available.

AR-15-style rifles are a favorite among many three-gun competitors.

Chapter 18: Rifle Shooting Activities

Various types of targets may be presented to a shooter in three-gun competition.

Three-gun matches, such as those sanctioned by the NRA, the *International Practical Shooting Confederation (IPSC)*, or by individual gun clubs, involve shooting stages using a centerfire pistol, centerfire rifle and 12-gauge shotgun. Some stages require the use of only one gun, while in others the shooter must engage targets with two or all three guns. Competitors usually have to move between firing points, engaging multiple targets from behind barricades and through shooting ports. Rifle targets in three-gun matches are generally reasonably close—200 yards or less; the AR-15 in .223 Rem., with iron, red-dot or telescopic sights is overall the most popular type of rifle used.

The second form of practical rifle shooting is *tactical rifle competition*. In these matches, targets may be set at as little as 50 yards to as far as 1,000 yards or more. Both steel shapes and humanoid cardboard targets may be used, and are often placed at unknown distances to test the shooters' range-estimation skills. Moving targets, disappearing targets, and camouflaged or partially hidden targets may be presented, at different ranges, which the shooter must often engage from improvised or difficult shooting positions.

Precision is needed when firing at targets at 1,000 yards, making bolt-action rifles the overwhelming choice of tactical rifle competitors (except in matches limited to semi-automatic rifles). Among the most popular calibers are the .308 Winchester, 6.5 Creedmoor, .260 Rem. and .243 Win.

Also required are rugged variable scope sights with mil-dot or other types of rangefinding reticles for targets at unknown distances. Useful accessories for tactical rifle shooting include slings, wind gauges and (for matches in which they are allowed) laser rangefinders.

SILHOUETTE COMPETITION

In *silhouette shooting,* the targets are life-size or reduced-size steel silhouettes of four game animals—ram, turkey, pig and chicken—that must be knocked over to score a hit. Banks of targets for each animal are set at different distances from the firing line. In classes for centerfire rifle calibers, the chicken, pig, turkey and ram targets are placed at 200, 300, 385 and 500 yards (or meters), respectively. Target distances are reduced for smallbore and air rifles.

Competition is held in a wide variety of classes, including high power and high power hunting silhouette rifles; high power semi-automatic military rifle; smallbore and smallbore hunting silhouette rifles, and three classes of silhouette air rifle competition. There are also three classes for cowboy lever-action rifles, as well as for black powder cartridge rifles, both scoped and with iron sights. Scopes are allowed except in the classes for semi-automatic military rifles, cowboy lever guns, and iron-sighted black powder cartridge rifles.

Rifle silhouette targets represent game animals, placed in banks of five at different distances.

Shooting is done from the standing position, with the exception that black powder cartridge rifles, with iron or scope sights, may be fired from any position with the use of crossed sticks for support.

COWBOY ACTION COMPETITION

Cowboy Action Shooting reflects an interest in the historical American West. Cowboy Action competitors are required to dress in period clothing and assume nicknames reflecting the flavor of the Old West. Most matches have events for rifles, pistols and shotguns.

Courses of fire often replicate scenarios typical of the Old West, and reflect the originality and creativity of the course designer. Thus, the stages at each match are likely to be very different. Extensive use is made of period props, such as barrels, hay bales, and even small buildings to give the shooter new and interesting challenges. Successful Cowboy Action rifle shooters must be able to fire from a variety of positions, at ranges up to 50 yards.

Targets include metal plates, cardboard silhouettes and other safe objects as appropriate. Scoring is calculated on the basis of both the hits achieved and the time taken to complete the stage.

Rifles for Cowboy Action Shooting are limited to those guns (or modern copies) whose designs originated prior to approximately 1900. Most popular are 19th-century lever-action rifles (or reproductions), as these are quick-handling, sufficiently accurate and offer a rapid rate of fire.

Cowboy Action shooters have an extensive range of accessories from which to choose, from period clothes, boots and hats to various types of holsters, gun belts, cartridge belts and more.

BENCHREST COMPETITION

Benchrest competition involves firing a rifle off a bench, supported front and rear by sandbag rests, at bullseyes or specialized benchrest targets. Benchrest shooting places an extraordinary premium on rifle accuracy, and benchrest guns are among the most accurate in the world.

Conventional benchrest matches are fired most often at 100 and 200 yards (although 300-yard and even 600-yard matches are also held). Matches may be shot for group or

CHAPTER 19
Additional Opportunities for Skill Development

The NRA Basic Rifle Course should not be regarded as the endpoint of the training experience, but rather as the first step in the development of rifle shooting skills and abilities. There are many ways in which the knowledge, skills and attitude that are acquired in the Basic Rifle Course can be enhanced, from individual practice to formal training and official competition. The selection of the appropriate activity is based on your needs, resources and time schedule.

DRY-FIRE PRACTICE

Dry-fire practice is an inexpensive, safe and time-efficient way to enhance shooting fundamentals and practice the various shooting positions. Dry-firing involves practicing every phase of the firing process using an *unloaded* firearm.

All dry-fire practice must be performed under the following safety rules:

- The firearm must be completely unloaded
- All dry-firing is done in a dedicated dry-fire area having a safe backstop at which the gun is pointed
- No live ammunition is allowed in the dedicated dry-fire area
- Reloading drills are performed only with dummy ammunition

Of course, even though the firearm is unloaded, it is important to still observe the first Rule for Safe Gun Handling—**ALWAYS keep the gun pointed in a safe direction.**

Dry-firing can be used to master the various shooting positions, adjust a sling, improve strength and position stability, and, of course, practice the shooting fundamentals as well as grip and NPA (Natural Point of Aim). The ways that dry-firing can be used to enhance shooting skills are limited only by the imagination.

Laser technology affords a variation on traditional dry-fire techniques, in the form of target systems allowing an unmodified firearm to "fire" a beam of laser light at a target sensor. Such systems use a cartridge-shaped laser light inserted into the gun's chamber and activated by the firing pin strike.

A laser can also be used in conjunction with dry-fire practice to improve the steadiness with which the rifle is held in various positions. To do this, the laser is mounted on the barrel near the muzzle and aligned so that its dot is closely aligned with the aiming point seen through the sights. The laser is turned on and the shooter assumes the firing position and goes through the steps of the shot process, typically aiming at a target on a wall. Gun movement will be reflected in the position of the red dot on the target.

LIVE-FIRE PRACTICE

Although dry-fire practice, as well as the review of books, videos and other materials, can add considerably to your knowledge and ability, there is no substitute for live-fire practice in improving rifle shooting skills. Initially, the novice shooter should concentrate upon drills that promote mastery of the shooting fundamentals. Later, as skill improves, more challenging drills may be practiced.

The effectiveness of live-fire practice can be enhanced by a shooting partner.

A shooting partner during live-fire exercises not only provides an additional incentive to practice; such a partner can help you better assess your progress. During a live-fire practice session, a partner can observe and give feedback on position and shooting fundamentals. On occasion a video record of the practice session may be useful in perfecting form or diagnosing shooting problems, particularly when played back in slow motion. The video camera must always be placed at or behind the firing line, never in front of the muzzle. In the absence of a partner, the camera may be placed on a tripod and operated remotely.

WINCHESTER/NRA RIFLE MARKSMANSHIP QUALIFICATION PROGRAM

Any rifle shooter can develop skills and gain recognition for his or her level of proficiency in the Winchester/NRA Rifle Marksmanship Qualification Program, a self-paced recreational shooting activity that provides shooters of all skill levels with both fun and a sense of accomplishment. The program consists of seven different skill ratings which are earned by attaining the required scores on a series of increasingly challenging courses of fire. For more information on the Winchester/NRA Rifle Marksmanship Qualification Program, visit: mqp.nra.org

ADDITIONAL TRAINING

The NRA Basic Rifle Course provides a thorough grounding in the fundamentals of safe and effective rifle shooting. Practice and application of these techniques will greatly enhance rifle shooting skill and enjoyment.

Individuals wishing to improve performance in specific types of rifle competition may avail themselves of the knowledge and experience of an NRA Coach. Coaches are available nationwide in all NRA-sanctioned rifle disciplines, including High Power, Smallbore, Silhouette, and Air Rifle. An NRA Coach can enhance the skill of any rifle shooter, from beginning competitors to national-level champions. For more information, contact the NRA Coach Program at coaching@nrahq.org

Some shooters may wish to avail themselves of non-NRA training available at numerous facilities throughout the country. The instruction provided at such facilities may vary in terms of length, quality, type and cost. Shooters contemplating enrolling at such a facility should consider:

- Reputation of facility
- Geographic location
- Cost of course
- Credentials of instructors
- Student-teacher ratio
- Safety record of institution
- Types of courses offered
- Availability of nearby lodging (for multi-day courses)

PART V

RIFLE SELECTION AND MAINTENANCE

CHAPTER 20
Selecting Rifles, Ammunition and Accessories

Today's rifle buyer has an unprecedented range of choices of rifle manufacturers, models, action types and calibers, not to mention ammunition and accessories. This can be confusing, especially for the first-time gun buyer. For such an individual, a logical selection process is needed.

SELECTING A RIFLE
Stage I: Research

Before the research process is even started, the following question should be answered by anyone thinking of buying a rifle: *Am I a sufficiently responsible person to own a firearm?* While gun ownership is a constitutionally guaranteed right in the United States, there are still those who lack the maturity, emotional stability, or willingness to accept the responsibility of gun ownership. Anyone who recognizes this in him- or herself, and chooses not to own a firearm, should be commended for their responsible decision.

For those who elect to own a rifle, the single most important selection criterion revolves around the *purpose* of the firearm. In some cases, there will be a single clear-cut reason for rifle ownership—formal target shooting, hunting, or home protection, for example. The identification of this reason greatly simplifies rifle selection.

Many shooters, however, intend to use a rifle for a number of activities. Although some rifles are suitable for more than one shooting purpose, any claim that one rifle will do everything should be met with skepticism. Most multipurpose guns embody a series of compromises that may make them mediocre, at best, for any single function. The shooter wishing to engage in several different shooting activities will usually end up with a separate gun for each activity, or a single gun that is best suited for the highest-priority purpose.

The *action type* of the desired rifle should also be considered at this stage. Sometimes the action type will be determined by the purpose. The bolt-action rifle, for example, is the strongest, most accurate and simplest type of rifle action, and is thus preferred by many target

Rifles for different purposes, including recreational shooting, hunting, and NRA High Power, Cowboy Action and silhouette competition. Above, five different rifles used for different applications.

shooters and hunters. The simplicity of this type of action also makes it ideal for new shooters. Magazine capacity of most models is limited, however, and each shot requires manually working the action.

Shooters wanting faster follow-up shots or greater magazine capacity may select the semi-automatic rifle. Some of these resemble military-style rifles, while others are similar in appearance to conventional hunting rifles. Semi-automatics are generally not as reliable nor as accurate as bolt-action guns, and are more complex to operate. However, because these rifles utilize some of the energy produced upon firing to work the action, they generate slightly less recoil than bolt-action rifles of the same weight, in the same caliber.

The lever-action rifle is a reliable, proven and familiar design, and is frequently the choice of deer hunters in the woods. Lever-action guns allow more rapid shooting than bolt-action rifles, but tend to be not as accurate. Furthermore, the limited strength of the lever-action design often restricts it to cartridges of lower power than used in bolt-action or even semi-automatic rifles. As was mentioned in Chapter 17: Rifle Shooting Activities, lever-action rifles are also required for some shooting activities, such as Cowboy Action Shooting.

Finally, the slide-action rifle offers reasonably quick follow-up shots, and may be preferred by those already accustomed to hunting with a pump-action shotgun.

The prospective gun buyer, in the research stage, should also look into the reputation of the manufacturer and model of any rifle under consideration. Usually, the best choice is a standard model of proven design, made by an established, reputable gunmaker. Recently introduced or innovative designs from new gun companies should probably be avoided.

The rifle's materials may also influence the selection process. At one time all guns were made of steel and wood; now, titanium and aluminum alloys, as well as polymer materials, are commonplace. As a general rule, steel is still the strongest material, and is the basis for the vast majority of rifle barrels, receivers. and critical action parts. Steel, however, is also heavy and can corrode, while aluminum, titanium and polymers do not corrode to any appreciable extent. Some rifles have aluminum or titanium receivers; these are serviceable and light, and most rifle owners will not shoot enough to see a difference in longevity between steel and any other material. Because of their reduced weight, titanium, aluminum and polymer materials are often used in lightweight hunting rifles, particularly models used for mountain hunting. There is a downside to such materials, however, as easy-to-carry lightweight guns give more recoil than heavier, all-steel firearms of the same size.

A final, crucial factor to be researched is *safety*. While modern firearms from reputable manufacturers are generally over-engineered, with multiple safety features built in, some designs may confer an additional margin of safety in certain situations, such as in households where there are children or others not authorized to use or handle the firearm. As an example of this, the bolt on a bolt-action rifle may easily be removed and stored separately from the rest of the gun, rendering the bolt-less rifle inoperable. Also, some rifles incorporate key-operated action locks in their designs that, when activated, prevent firing. The prospective gun buyer should weigh such features, and the inherent safety of each action type, in light of his or her own particular living situation. Some safety features may compromise rapid rifle deployment in an emergency situation.

As a general rule, the novice rifle owner is best with a new firearm having a full warranty, rather than a used model whose previous history of use or abuse may be unknown. An exception might be made for a used rifle sold and warranted by a reputable gun dealer.

A variety of information resources can be consulted in the research phase, including books, magazines, gun dealers, gun clubs and the internet (see Appendix D: Information and Training Resources).

Stage II: Examination

Once the research stage has narrowed the range of choices down to a handful of models, the prospective gun buyer should examine these choices in a gun shop.

Here, the shooter may learn much about each model—how it balances in the hand and mounts to the shoulder, how smoothly and easily the action cycles, how large and heavy it is, the ease with which its controls may be manipulated and so forth. With the help of a knowledgeable store clerk, the gun buyer can go through the operations required to load, unload, and fire the firearm, using an empty gun.

Gun fit is an important factor in rifle selection, and is largely subjective. Small differences in pistol grip shape, buttstock length and comb height may radically alter the feel of the gun on the shoulder. For each shooter there is an ideal *trigger pull length* (the distance from the trigger face to the end of the buttpad); this varies with arm length, neck length, head position and more. Trigger pull lengths that are too long or too short will place the shooter in an unnatural shooting position that will inhibit good shooting. Some rifles have buttstocks that are adjustable for length of pull, to address this problem.

Also important is the physical strength or coordination required to operate the rifle. Some people may have difficulty retracting the bolt handle of a semi-automatic rifle with a stiff recoil spring, or quickly working a lever-action or pump-action rifle. Cycling the action of an empty gun in a gun shop is a good way for you to determine if a particular gun and action type is easy to operate.

Cost and quality are also factors. While low-price models may be appealing, they can represent false economy if they fail to provide the desired reliability, durability or accuracy. The price and availability of ammunition, parts, accessories and so forth should also be considered. Also, certain models are supplied with a greater number of aftermarket parts and accessories, or may be easier for a gunsmith to work on.

Through the process outlined above the prospective gun buyer should be able to further narrow the number of potential choices.

Stage III: Test Firing

The final stage in the rifle selection process involves test-firing representative samples of the remaining viable choices. This often may be accomplished at ranges having rifles for rent, or used rifles for sale that interested customers may try. In this activity, the individual can judge the recoil, accuracy, comfort and feel of each. Any stoppages or other problems can be noted.

Semi-automatic rifles should be fired with both a tight and a loose grip, and with the ejection port facing both upward and downward. When the rifle is held in the normal vertical position, with the ejection port facing to the side, ejection should be strong, with cases landing at least six feet to the right of the gun. Loads of different levels of power and with different bullet shapes should also be tried, and each magazine of a prospective purchase should be tested.

With all rifle types, firing pin indentations should be deep and round. Recoil and accuracy should be evaluated with various loads. Adjustable sights should be evaluated to ensure that sight adjustments are crisp, repeatable and accurate.

Finally, the test-fire session will assist the gun buyer determine the choice of the appropriate caliber. Many gun models are produced in a variety of chamberings. A typical bolt-action hunting rifle for deer hunting, for example, may be available in .243 Winchester, .270 Winchester, .308 Winchester and .30-'06 Springfield. These cartridges are all effective on deer-size game, but can vary distinctly in recoil. A range session will help the new rifle buyer decide upon a chambering with an acceptable level of recoil.

SELECTING RIFLE AMMUNITION AND ACCESSORIES

Accuracy, reliability and other aspects of rifle performance depend at least as much upon the ammunition chosen as on the particular gun design. Also, even after the proper gun and ammunition are chosen, a variety of rifle accessories can further enhance a shooter's enjoyment and performance in any shooting activity.

SELECTING RIFLE AMMUNITION

The selection of the proper ammunition type and load involves consideration of several factors, among the most important of which are: *safety, purpose, reliability, accuracy,* and *recoil.*

Safety— Ammunition safety primarily involves using the proper ammunition for the firearm. As described in Chapter 9: Ammunition Fundamentals, this is accomplished by matching the caliber designation on the barrel and/or slide with that on the ammunition package and cartridge headstamp.

As a general rule, the novice rifle owner should avoid reloaded ammunition, as well as military surplus ammunition, and purchase only new ammunition from a reputable manufacturer.

Purpose— The intended purpose of the rifle/ammunition combination is the main factor in determining the choice of caliber, cartridge power, and bullet weight, design and construction. For example, target shooting, hunting and home protection all require different types of ammunition.

Information on the general ammunition types required for different rifle shooting activities can be found in many gun books, magazines and videos.

Reliability— Reliability is the ability of a load to consistently feed, fire, eject and cycle the action. Reliability issues most often plague semi-automatic rifles, although certain types of problems may be seen with all action types. Factors that can influence ammunition reliability include load power, bullet shape, cartridge overall length, crimp and much more. In general, any load used in a critical application should be absolutely reliable during a test of at least 100 rounds.

Persistent reliability problems with various loads may indicate a situation that must require resolution by a gunsmith.

Accuracy— Accuracy—the ability of a firearm and ammunition to reliably hit the target—is a function of several factors: the gun, the load used, and the skill of the shooter. The level of accuracy required in different activities can vary greatly. Information on the accuracy needed in various rifle shooting activities can be found in various books, magazines and videos.

Accuracy testing should ideally involve a number of five- or 10-shot groups fired from a bench-rest position at a target placed at an appropriate distance (see Chapter 12: The Benchrest Position).

Recoil— The recoil or "kick" felt by the shooter upon firing a gun will vary with gun weight, cartridge power, bullet weight, stock design, and more. Shooters also differ in their sensitivity to recoil. Excessive recoil can produce flinching or other problems that impair accurate shooting.

Determining the recoil a shooter can tolerate is usually made by test-firing different guns in different calibers. Novice shooters should avoid hard-kicking rifles, as early exposure to high levels of recoil can cause flinching, shot anticipation, jerking the trigger and other unwanted habits. Note that many cartridges come in several loads of varying recoil, including "reduced recoil" loads that give nearly the same ballistic performance as standard loads, but with noticeably less recoil.

SELECTING RIFLE ACCESSORIES

Various types of rifle accessories can add greatly to one's enjoyment of any rifle shooting activity, as well as contributing to better shooting performance.

Eye and *hearing protection* are perhaps the most important accessories a shooter must have (see Chapter 1: Basic Firearm Safety).

A *range bag* of leather, canvas or nylon allows convenient carry and storage of ammunition, eye and hearing protection, targets and other items. A lockable *gun case* of fabric, synthetic materials or aluminum is essential for transporting the rifle to and from the range or hunting field, as is a *padlock* for securing the case.

The range bag should include a small *tool kit* containing, at a minimum, the items used for disassembling the rifle; a field *cleaning kit* (see Chapter 20: Cleaning and Maintaining Your Rifle); a small *first aid kit*, a *stapler* for mounting targets on the target frame, and *targets* and *target pasters*.

Various rifle accessories, including range bag, gun case, magazines and magazine loader, targets, first-aid kit, tool kit, sandbags and spotting scope

Chapter 20: Selecting Rifles, Ammunition and Accessories   123

For semi-automatic rifles, additional *magazines* are mandatory, as they can be easily damaged, even in normal use. Factory or high-quality aftermarket magazines should be favored over inexpensive "no-name" units, which may not function properly. Note that some rifles function better with one brand of magazine than another. Loading semi-automatic rifle magazines to full capacity is made easier with another accessory, the *magazine loader*.

Many rifle accessories are *aftermarket parts*, which can improve a rifle's ergonomics, reliability and accuracy. Examples of such parts include sights, triggers, safeties and bolt releases, match-grade barrels, springs and different types of stocks. A gunsmith should be consulted regarding the selection and installation of any such parts.

Rifle targets come in a variety of sizes, shapes and colors. While rifle competitors will use the targets of their particular discipline, recreational shooters have a variety of targets for practice, testing and plinking. *Target pasters* cover bullet holes in the target, extending target life.

An important accessory for many types of shooting is a *telescopic sight*. These come in magnifications from 2X to 60X, with 4 to 24X being most common, and may be of *fixed power* (one magnification) or *variable power* (a range of magnifications) design.

Such sights are used by aligning a *reticle* (aiming pattern) inside the scope with the target. Many reticle designs are available for specific purposes such as target shooting, hunting, range estimation and other purposes; most are a variation on the familiar crosshair. Knobs on the scope move the reticle in the horizontal and vertical directions, allowing the shooter to adjust the scope to hit targets at different ranges. In addition to providing magnification, telescopic sights serve to put the target and the reticle in the same focal or visual plane, making aiming easier. Also important are *mount* and *rings* for attaching the scope to the rifle, and *scope covers* to protect glass surfaces.

Telescopic sights and red-dot optics place the target and aiming point in the same focal plane, and are thus easier for some shooters to use.

For relatively short-range use, *red-dot sights* perform much the same function as telescopic sights, but offer no magnification and use a brightly illuminated dot as the aiming point rather than a crosshair.

Steadying the rifle as much as possible is a must for accurate shooting, and several accessories can assist with this. A *sling* can be used in several positions to reduce unwanted gun movement (see Appendix A: Using the Sling), as well as to carry the rifle in the field. *Bipods* for rifles are usually lightweight, reasonably rigid, and adjustable for height. Virtually all models fold against the stock for easy carry. *Rifle rests* of all types are available, from simple sandbags to highly precise front tripod rests that are vertically and horizontally adjustable. In activities requiring maximum accuracy, such as benchrest shooting, a precise tripod rest is used in conjunction with a special rear bag (see Chapter 17: Rifle Shooting Activities).

Depending upon the shooting activity, other accessories may also be useful. Taming the recoil of hard-kicking rifles is made possible through the use of a *recoil pad* that fits over the clothing. A *spotting scope* allows bullet holes to be seen in a distant target; a *chronograph* measures bullet muzzle velocity, which is crucial to the calculation of bullet energy and trajectory; and a *shooting timer* is used for shooting practice or competitions conducted under time limits.

CHAPTER 21
Cleaning and Maintaining Your Rifle

A gun that is regularly fired accumulates dirt, powder residue and other foreign matter, all of which can make it more prone to stoppage, wear and corrosion. Even a firearm that is left untouched in a gun rack or cabinet can accumulate sufficient dust and rust to affect functioning. Responsible gun owners understand that removing such material is critical to ensure gun reliability and readiness. A gun that is properly maintained at regular intervals—including cleaning, inspection and lubrication, as well as a periodic gunsmith check-up—will function more reliably, shoot more accurately and last longer than one where gun care is neglected.

Every gun owner should have a gun cleaning kit consisting of:

- cloth patches of the proper size for the bore;
- a cleaning rod and cleaning rod attachments, including a bore brush and tips or *jags* to hold patches;
- a small brush (for cleaning gun crevices) ;
- gun solvent (bore cleaner);
- gun oil; and
- a soft cloth.

Kits containing all or most of these items are commercially available at any gun shop and many hardware, sporting goods and large discount stores. Make sure that any such

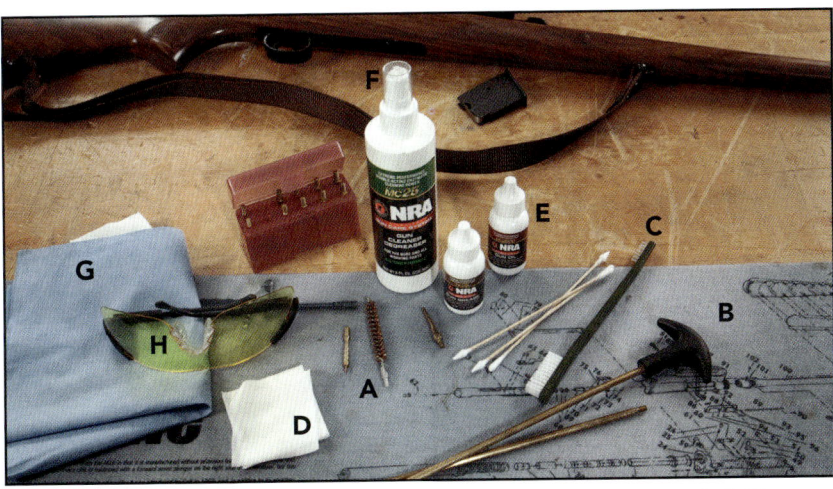

The components of a basic gun cleaning kit, including: (A) a bore brush and jags for holding cleaning patches, (B) a cleaning rod, (C) a small brush, (D) cotton cleaning patches, (E) gun oil, (F) gun cleaning solvent, (G) a soft cloth, and (H) eye protection. Also used are thin rubber gloves (not shown), which may help protect the skin from dirt, oil and solvent.

Chapter 21: Cleaning and Maintaining Your Rifle

kit, or any individual cleaning rod, jag (a tip designed specifically to hold a cleaning patch) or bore brush is the proper size for your rifle's caliber. The cloth patches should also be of the proper size.

Rifle in a gun cradle

Additionally, you need safety glasses to protect your eyes from cleaning solvents and spring-loaded parts that may be inadvertently released from your gun. Also recommended are thin rubber gloves to protect your skin from exposure to solvents, lubricants, firing residues and lead particles. Also useful, but not mandatory, is a gun cleaning *cradle* or *rest* that holds the rifle horizontally, making cleaning more convenient.

Be sure that your gun-cleaning area has good ventilation, and do not eat, drink or smoke while performing firearm cleaning or maintenance.

The first step in cleaning your firearm is to ensure that it is unloaded. **No ammunition should be in the cleaning area** (A).

Next, disassemble your firearm according to the instructions in the owner's manual for the gun. In many cases, complete disassembly is not required; simply removing the bolt

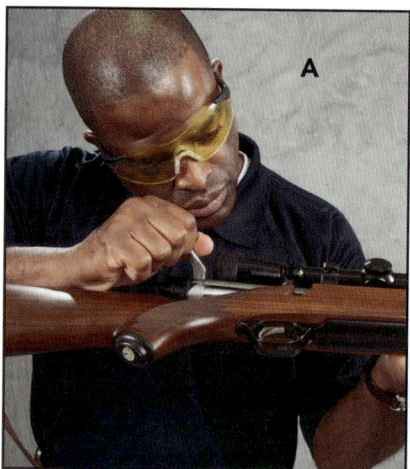

from a bolt-action rifle, for example, may be sufficient. If you do not have an owner's manual, you can usually obtain one from your gun's manufacturer (B). Also, a professional gunsmith may be able to show you how to disassemble your gun.

Attach the bore brush to the cleaning rod and moisten it with gun cleaning solvent (C). If possible, use a dropper or spray to put solvent onto the brush; avoid dipping the brush in the solvent, as this contaminates the clean solvent with dirt and grit that may be on the brush.

Push the brush all the way through the bore, then pull it back through. Whenever possible, the brush (and all patches) should

be pushed through from the breech end to the muzzle (D); this minimizes wear on the *crown*, the end of the rifling at the muzzle, and an area critical for best accuracy. However, with many rifles, such as most semi-automatic and pump-action rifles, and many lever-actions, this is not possible. With these

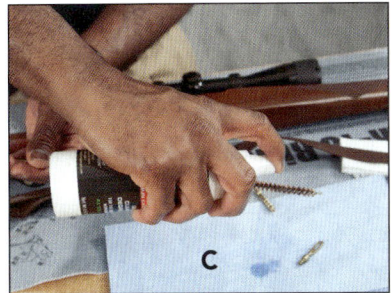

guns, the brush must be carefully inserted into the muzzle. An accessory called a *muzzle protector* can help keep the cleaning rod from causing wear on the crown.

Even when it is possible to insert the bore brush into the breech end of the barrel, as with bolt-action rifles, it is still desirable to minimize rubbing of the cleaning rod against the rifling, particularly in the *throat*, the area just forward of the chamber. A *bore guide* can keep the cleaning rod centered in the bore and away from the rifling.

Do not try to reverse direction with the brush still in the bore. Run the brush through the bore about 10-15 times, adding solvent to it as necessary.

Wipe the cleaning rod clean of excess solvent or residue, and then attach the jag to the cleaning rod (E) and push one or two patches moistened with solvent through the bore (F). These will come out quite dirty with the material that was loosened by the solvent and the bore brush. Run several dry patches through the bore. These should come out progressively cleaner, until virtually no fouling is visible. If the patches keep coming out somewhat dirty, repeat the cleaning process as outlined above. Visually check the bore for any remaining fouling, lead, or powder residue.

Once the bore is clean, residue must be removed from other gun components. Use a solvent-soaked patch, cotton swab or toothbrush, as appropriate, to loosen and remove powder residue and other matter from the bolt or breech block, the inside of the receiver, and all action parts that are accessible after disassembly (G). In some cases, special tools may be used to clean hard-to-get-at areas such as the locking recesses for the bolt.

In most cases, the owner's manual will present only basic disassembly instructions for general cleaning and maintenance; further gun disassembly by the owner is usually discouraged. However, dirt and powder residue collects in interior action areas that can be accessed only by complete disassembly. A partial cleaning of these areas may be achieved by flushing the action with a solvent that leaves no residue, such as some gun cleaners and automotive brake cleaner. The solvent is sprayed into the action in such a way as to allow the excess to drain freely, dissolving

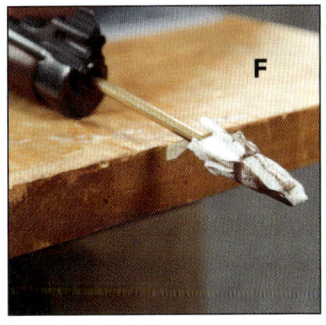

Chapter 21: Cleaning and Maintaining Your Rifle

and flushing away loosened dirt and residue (H). This process is particularly useful when cleaning trigger mechanisms, which may fail to function properly or safely if they harbor excess dirt or powder residue, or even congealed gun oil. Be sure the stock is removed before flushing the action with any solvent, as some solvents may damage the stock finish.

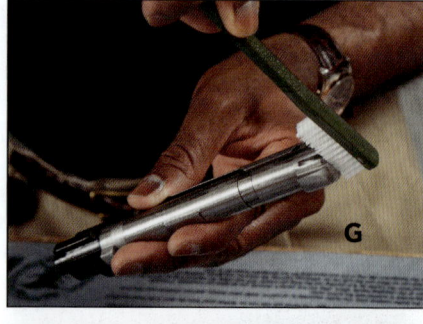

Use a soft cloth moistened with solvent to take dirt, gunpowder residue and surface rust off the exterior surfaces of the gun (I). Wipe the gun's exterior with a dry, clean cloth to remove any trace of solvent, and then follow this with a soft, lightly oiled cloth. A lightly oiled patch should also be run through the bore, particularly in humid environments or if the gun is to be stored for any appreciable period of time.

Maintenance of rifle magazines is critical for proper rifle functioning. Most magazines are designed to be disassembled; instructions should be in your owner's manual. Once the magazine is disassembled, remove dirt and powder residue from the inside of the magazine body using a brush and patches, or flush with a solvent as described above.

INSPECTING YOUR FIREARM

The ideal time for giving your firearm a thorough visual inspection is when it is disassembled after cleaning. Defects are easiest to spot on parts that are free of dirt, residue and oil. Look for cracks, burred, pitted or indented areas, broken components and so forth. Also be aware of screws or pins that have worked loose, sights that have drifted from recoil forces, or parts that seem to have shifted from their normal positions.

Additionally, every time you pick up your firearm, whether to practice at the range, dry-fire in your basement, or clean it in your workroom, you should give it a cursory inspection (after, of course, making sure it is unloaded). Look for the buildup of firing residue; stock screws or other parts that have become loose; excessive oil leaking out of the joints between parts; and any other condition that may adversely affect the functioning of the gun. Getting in the habit of making this kind of inspection will help you determine when cleaning or lubrication is necessary, or if there are any conditions that may make your gun unsafe or unreliable.

LUBRICATING YOUR FIREARM

Cleaning powder residues and other foreign material from the gun usually removes necessary lubrication from working surfaces. Thus, it is essential to re-lubricate the firearm after it has been cleaned.

The owner's manual for your gun will likely contain detailed instructions on the proper method of lubrication. In general, use a light gun oil on triggers, hammers, bolts and breech blocks, and most other action parts. Heavier lubricants, such as grease, should be used sparingly, and only on components where there may be a high degree of wear, such as on bolt lugs or other sliding surfaces.

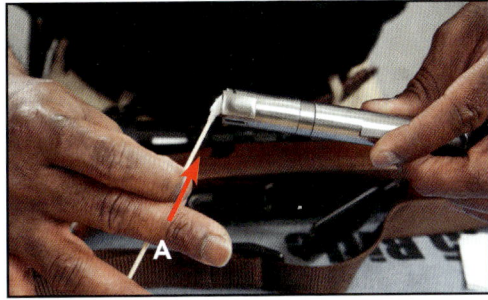

Rifle lubrication points include the body of the bolt (A) or breech block (B), the inside of the receiver and other areas where parts contact each other under pressure.

A very light film of oil may be put on the exterior surface of the rifle's magazines to prevent rust. However, it is critical not to allow oil to be transferred to the cartridges carried within the magazine. Oil or solvents on cartridge cases can penetrate to the primer, making its ignition unreliable, and may have other harmful effects on gun functioning as well.

Use only those lubricants designed expressly for use in firearms. Over time, improper lubricants may become gummy, impairing proper gun functioning, or may be too thin or runny to provide lasting protection. Also, firearms that are used in climates that are extremely hot, cold, wet or dusty often have very special lubrication needs, as do firearms that will be stored for extended periods. Consult with a gun shop or gunsmith to determine the proper lubricants to be used with your firearm.

It is also important to avoid over-lubricating your rifle, or leaving oil in certain areas. For example, while a thin film of oil should coat the bore of a firearm that is to be stored, all oil should be removed from the bore before the gun is fired. Excess lubricant can also penetrate wood stocks and cause them to deteriorate. Too much oil left on the exterior of a rifle that is carried in a leather scabbard can soak into the leather, softening it. And, as explained above, oil left inside the magazine of a semi-automatic rifle can contaminate cartridge primers and lead to misfires.

FUNCTION CHECKING YOUR FIREARM

After cleaning, inspecting and lubricating the firearm, the final stage is reassembly and function checking. During reassembly, be aware of parts that do not go together as they should, a sudden increase in the play or looseness of pins and other components. Ensure that the proper torque is used on areas such as stock screws and sight bases The loosening of such screws is a common cause of a sudden loss of accuracy.

When the firearm is reassembled, make sure that it is unloaded and then cycle the action and dry-fire it a few times to see if there are any changes in gun operation. (Note that .22 rimfire rifles, and some centerfire rifles, should only be dry-fired with a dummy shell or "snap cap" in the chamber.) Check to make sure that all controls, such as safeties, magazine releases, and bolt stops function properly. When doing such testing, be alert to any change in the way the gun looks, feels, and even sounds. Sometimes the sound of the gun as it is cycled or dry-fired can reveal a functional problem.

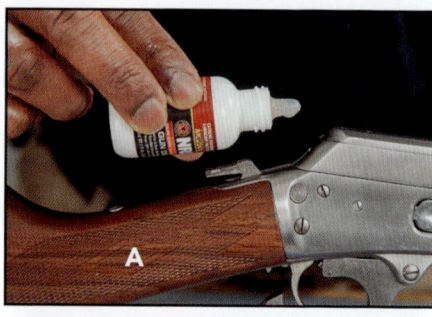
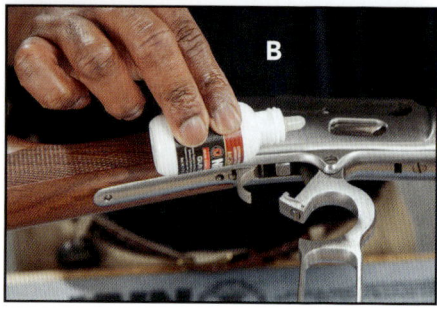

Lubricate the hammer (A) and lever mechanism (B) of lever-action rifles, and the slide components.

Similarly, when firing live ammunition at the range, be aware of any changes in the gun's function or feel. Gradual changes in gun function such as sluggish cycling, frequent stoppages or larger groups can result from a buildup of dirt, bullet jacket or gunpowder residue or congealed lubricant. Thorough cleaning and lubrication often restores proper functioning in such cases. However, a sudden tendency of the gun to misfire, jam, or change the size or location of its groups may be a sign of a broken part or other serious mechanical problem that usually requires gunsmith attention.

OTHER MAINTENANCE

Firearm maintenance involves more than just cleaning, inspection, lubrication and function testing. All types of rifles are powered by springs, which can, over time, fatigue. The springs that power firing pins or hammers normally last for many years; however, they may be suspect in any rifle having a tendency to produce light hits on the primer.

Weakening of the recoil springs on semi-automatic rifles is more common, and such springs should be regularly replaced. Your owner's manual, or a competent gunsmith, should be able to provide recommendations regarding recoil spring replacement, as well as directions for installing new springs. Magazine springs, too, sometimes require replacement, as they can lose stiffness over time (particularly when left compressed) and produce feeding problems. A competent gunsmith can diagnose and remedy problems stemming from fatigued springs.

For some highly popular guns, such as bolt-action or AR-15-type rifles, there are factory or aftermarket parts, or even parts kits, that allow the replacement of components that often wear with use. Many of these can be installed by the mechanically-inclined owner. However, any such repair should be checked by a gunsmith familiar with the particular rifle model.

GUNSMITH CHECK-UP

In addition to the normal maintenance you can perform, it is important to periodically have a gunsmith completely disassemble, clean, inspect and lubricate your firearm. This is also an opportunity for an experienced eye to look for wear, breakage or other conditions that may affect your gun's ability to function properly.

The frequency of this kind of gunsmith examination depends upon your shooting habits. In general, if you regularly hunt, compete or practice with your rifle, an annual check-up is recommended.

APPENDIXES

APPENDIX A
Using the Sling

USING THE SLING

The rifle sling is a useful accessory for carrying the rifle in the field. Even more importantly, however, a sling, properly used, can greatly increase the stability of any shooting position.

When hunting, target shooting or plinking, any type of rest supporting the rifle's fore-end will greatly aid the shooter with the challenging task of holding the rifle steady. In the prone, sitting and kneeling positions a sling is recommended to support the rifle so that the muscles of the arm won't have to. All formal target shooting in these positions is done with a sling to produce the highest possible stability and scores. Even during hunting, when you may have to shoot quickly, taking a few extra seconds to use a sling will return big dividends in making an accurate shot.

There are two types of slings that can be used for rifle support. A *hasty sling* is the term used when a conventional sling used for carrying a rifle is used for improvised support. A loop sling or cuff sling is designed specifically for target shooting, and also may be used for hunting situations when sufficient time is available. A loop sling takes more time to put on and adjust, but provides far more support than a hasty sling.

THE HASTY SLING

Shooter using a hasty sling

To use a hasty sling, the carry sling must have several inches of slack. With the rifle in the firing hand, the muzzle elevated, and the trigger finger outside the trigger guard alongside the stock, insert the support arm between the sling and the rifle up to the upper arm. Swing the hand and forearm outward in a circular motion so that the arm wraps around the sling, and place the support hand under the rifle's fore-end just behind the sling swivel. Bring the rifle to eye level and put the buttstock into the firing-hand shoulder.

A proper hasty sling wraps tightly over the back of the support hand, crosses the inside of the support-hand forearm, wraps around the upper part of the support arm and finally passes under the armpit to the rear sling swivel. Length adjustment of the sling is key. When properly adjusted, the sling will be tight around the support arm, and will pull the rifle firmly into the shoulder, reducing the amount of muscle tension required in the support arm to hold the gun.

Note that a different sling length may be needed to get the proper fit of the hasty sling in different positions.

Assuming a position with a hasty sling: Put the support arm between the sling and the rifle up to the upper arm (A). Swing the arm and forearm in a circular motion to wrap the arm around the sling (B). and place the support hand under the rifle's fore-end (C). Finally, raise the rifle to eye level and put the rifle butt into the shoulder (D). The sling should be tight around the back of the hand, the forearm and the upper arm.

THE LOOP SLING

The loop sling is commonly used in target shooting, and can also be used in hunting when sufficient time is available. It takes longer to put on but provides far more support than the hasty sling.

To put on a loop sling, first open the sling loop, and twist the loop clockwise one-quarter turn. (This is for a right-handed shooter; left-handed shooters should twist the loop counter-clockwise. Place the loop high on the support-hand arm, and then tighten the sling keeper, buckle or other tightening device until the loop is snug. Avoid overtightening the loop; this could reduce circulation to the arm.

Wrap the support arm around the sling using a clockwise circular movement (for right-handed shooters) so that the sling comes across the back of the support hand and forearm.

Get into position with the sling loosened. Adjust the sling length so that it, not the muscles of the support arm, holds the rifle in position against the shoulder. Once the sling is adjusted for length, it should not need to be readjusted each time the shooter gets into position.

Assuming a position with the loop sling: First, open the sling loop (A). Twist the loop one-quarter turn clockwise (for a right-handed shooter) (B). For a left-handed shooter, the loop should be given a quarter-turn twist in the counter-clockwise direction. Place the loop high on the upper support-hand arm (C). Finally, raise the rifle to eye level and put the rifle butt into the shoulder (D).

APPENDIX B
Using the Shotgun as a Rifle

Today an increasing number of shooters are using shotguns as rifles, firing shotgun ammunition called *slugs*. A shotgun slug is a single projectile loaded in a shotgun shell, and is similar in principle to to the bullet in a metallic cartridge.

Much of the interest in slug shooting has been caused by new hunting laws in many jurisdictions that limit big-game hunting to shotguns only. The shotgun slug gives better performance on game than even the largest buckshot.

There are two kinds of slugs: those made for smoothbore barrels, and those made for rifled barrels. The traditional smoothbore slug is the *rifled slug*, a solid lead projectile with angled grooves and ridges around its circumference that resemble the rifling in a barrel. These grooves and ridges do not cause the slug to spin, nor confer any ballistic advantage. The rifled slug's aerodynamic stability relies instead upon the fact that most of its weight is in the front, making it nose-heavy like a badminton shuttlecock. Rifled slugs can be fired through a shotgun barrel having any degree of choke, as the soft lead slug will conform to the hard steel of the barrel.   Because rifled slugs are not spin-stabilized, and have poor aerodynamic characteristics, they are limited in range to about 75 yards or so.

While the shotgun traditionally has a smooth bore, some today are made with rifled barrels, and fire slugs expressly designed for them. Some rifled-slugs are full-diameter, but contemporary shotgunners increasingly prefer *saboted slugs*. These consist of a smaller-than-bore-diameter projectile encased in a synthetic *sabot* or casing that fits snugly in the bore and engages the rifling. As the saboted slug travels down the bore, the rifling causes both the sabot and the slug inside it to spin, imparting stability. When the sabot and slug leave the bore, the sabot falls away, allowing the slug to continue downrange.

Saboted slugs are more accurate than rifled slugs, and can achieve much higher velocities, sometimes more than 2,000 f.p.s. Additionally, saboted slugs have shapes that cut through the air better than rifled slugs. As a result, saboted slugs fired out of highly accurate rifled-barrel slug guns have a range of up to 150 yards.

Though any shotgun can be used for slug shooting, for most hunting purposes 12- and 20-gauge guns are best. Semi-automatic and pump-action shotguns are most popular, but also available are rifled-bore bolt-action slug guns made for maximum accuracy. Many of these latter guns can rival hunting rifles for accuracy.

Slug guns usually have adjustable rifle-type sights rather than the bead typical of shotguns used to hunt birds.

Rifled (left) and saboted slugs

Some feature ghost-ring sights, which consist of a large rear aperture and front post. Unlike aperture rifle sights, which obscure everything except what can be seen through the small-diameter peep, ghost ring sights allow a more complete view of the target area. The ring itself is seen as a shadowy circle, hence the name "ghost ring." As with conventional peep sights, ghost ring sights rely upon the tendency of the eye to automatically center anything seen through the aperture.

Alternatively, slug guns may be equipped with red-dot or telescopic sights. Such sights are particularly useful with rifled-barrel slug guns capable of a high degree of accuracy.

Whatever type of slug gun is chosen, testing with a variety of slug loads is critical to obtaining the best accuracy. Slugs can vary greatly in performance from gun to gun.

Among some shooters, shotgun slugs have a reputation as "brush busters." In reality, all projectiles will be deflected to some degree by passage through heavy vegetation.

Although rifled shotgun slugs have an effective range of only 75 yards or so, they can travel more than 1,000 yards in the air. Some saboted slugs may travel even farther. All the rules of gun safety must be observed when shooting slugs.

APPENDIX C
Facts About the NRA

Established in 1871, the National Rifle Association of America (NRA) is a non-profit organization supported entirely by membership fees and by donations from public-spirited citizens.

The NRA does not receive any appropriations from Congress, nor is it a trade organization. It is not affiliated with any gun or ammunition manufacturers, or with any businesses which deal in guns or ammunition.

The membership roster of the NRA has included seven U.S. Presidents, two U.S. Supreme Court chief justices, and many of America's outstanding diplomats, military leaders, members of Congress, and other public officials.

Originally formed to promote marksmanship training, the NRA has since reached out to establish a wide variety of activities, ranging from gun safety programs for children and adults to gun collecting and gunsmithing.

Law enforcement personnel throughout the country have also received training from NRA Certified Law Enforcement Instructors in the firearm skills needed to protect themselves and the public.

In addition, clubs that are enrolled or affiliated with the NRA exist in communities across the nation, teaching youths and adults gun safety, marksmanship, and responsibility while also providing recreational activities.

The NRA cooperates with federal agencies, all branches of the U.S. Armed Forces, and state and local governments that are interested in training and safety programs.

The basic goals of the NRA are to:

- Protect and defend the Constitution of the United States, especially in regard to the Second Amendment-protected right of the individual citizen to keep and bear arms.
- Promote public safety, law and order, and the national defense.
- Train citizens and members of law enforcement agencies and the armed forces in the safe handling and efficient use of firearms.
- Foster and promote the shooting sports at local, state regional, national, and international levels.
- Promote hunter safety and proper wildlife management.

For additional information about the NRA, including programs, publications and membership, contact: National Rifle Association of America, 11250 Waples Mill Road, Fairfax, VA 22030, (800) NRA-3888, www.nra.org.

Index

Aiming, 71
Ammunition, 59
  components, 59-61
  safety, 63-64
  selecting, 122
Balanced shooting position, 75
Barrel, 15
Benchrest position, 79-83
Blowback operation, 30
Bore, 13, 15
Breath control, 69
Breech, 13
Breech-loading firearms, 13
Bullet, 61
  types, 61
Cartridge, *see* Ammunition
Cartridge case, 59
Cartridge firing sequence, 62-63
Centerfire cartridge, 43
Chamber, 44
Cleaning a firearm, 127-130
Cleaning kit, 127
Clearing stoppages, 65
Comfortable shooting position, 77
Cycle of operation, *see* Firearm cycle of operation
Decocking
  pump-action rifles, 52
Dry-fire practice, 78, 113
  safety, 113

Dummy ammunition, 113
Eye dominance, 69-70
Eye dominance exercise, 69
Eye protection, 5
Firearm accessories, 122-125
Firearm cycle of operation, 17
  bolt-action rifle, 23
  semi-automatic rifle, 33
  lever-action rifle, 41
  slide-action rifle, 49
Firearm maintenance
  cleaning kit, 127
  cleaning process, 127-130
  cleaning rifle magazines, 129
  function-checking, 132
  inspection, 130
  lubrication, 131
  gunsmith checkup, 133
  other maintenance, 132
Firearm safety, 5
Firearm storage, 7-9
Firing
  bolt-action rifle, 27
  semi-automatic rifle, 36
  lever-action rifle, 44
  slide-action rifle, 52
Firing pin, 13
Firing sequence of a cartridge, 62
Fixed sights, 82
Follow-through, 69
Function checking a firearm, 132

Gas operation, 30
Grip, one-handed, 70
Grip, two-handed, 71
Gun cases, 8
Gun fit, 121
Gun owner's responsibility, x
Gunpowder, 13
Gun safes, 9
Gun safety, 3-9
Gunsmith checkup, 133
Gun storage, 9
Hearing protection, 5
Hold control, 69
Inspecting a firearm, 130
Jams, *see* Stoppages
Live-fire practice, 114
Loading
  bolt-action rifle, 25
  semi-automatic rifle, 34
  lever-action rifle, 43
  slide-action rifle, 50
  rifle magazines, 51
Loading gate, 43
Locked breech, 13, 15-16
Locking mechanisms (gun storage)
  keyed locks, 7
  combination locks, 7
  Simplex® locks, 7
Lubricating a firearm, 131-132
Magazines, rifle, 39
  cleaning, 130
  loading, 42-43

Magazines on firearm use, 121
Magazine release, 29
NPA, *see* Natural Point of Aim
National Rifle Association of America (NRA), 143
Natural Point of Aim (NPA), 76-77
  exercise, 77
NRA, *see* National Rifle Association of America
Rifle accessories, 119-125
Receiver, 15
Rifle action types
  bolt-action rifle, 19
  semi-automatic rifle, 29
  lever-action rifle, 39
  slide-action rifle, 47
Rifle aftermarket parts, 121
Rifle selection, 119-122
Positions - *see* Shooting positions
Powder, 13
Practice
  dry-fire practice, 113
  live-fire practice, 113
Primer, 60
Propellant, *see* Powder
Rimfire cartridge, 29
Safety
  fundamental rules for safe gun handling, 3
  rules for using or storing a gun, 4-6
  safe firearm storage, 7-9
Safety devices
  active, 15
  passive, 16
Selecting a rifle, 119-122

Selecting rifle accessories, 123-125
Selecting rifle ammunition, 122-123
Semi-automatic rifle
  blowback-operated, 30
  gas-operated, 30
  recoil-operated, 30
  magazines, 31
  operating, 33-38
  parts and operation, 29-38
Shooting accessories, 119-125
Shooting fundamentals, 78
Shooting position
  benchrest, 79
  elements of, 75
  standing, free arm, 85
  standing, arm rest, 85
  prone, 89
  kneeling, 93
  sitting, 97
  learning, 77-78
Sight adjustment, 82
Sight alignment, 87
Sight picture, 81
Sights, rifle
  adjustable, 81-82
  fixed
Simplex® locks, 7
Stoppages
  hangfire
  misfire
  squib load
  failure to fire
  causes, 127
Storage of firearms, 7-9
Striker, 14
Trigger control, 73
Trigger finger placement, 71
Unloading

bolt-action rifle, 27
semi-automatic rifle, 37
lever-action rifle, 45
slide-action rifle, 52
rifle magazines, 39
Winchester/NRA Rifle Marksmanship Qualification Program, 114

Index